MURDERS, MYSTERIES, AND MISDEMEANORS OF LAS VEGAS

MURDERS, MYSTERIES, AND MISDEMEANORS OF LAS VEGAS

JANICE OBERDING

AMERICA
THROUGH TIME®
ADDING COLOR TO AMERICAN HISTORY

For my two favorite Las Vegans—Bonnie Harper and Roy Harper,
Mom and Dad, whose love and knowledge of their city showed me the way

America Through Time is an imprint of Fonthill Media LLC
www.through-time.com
office@through-time.com

Published by Arcadia Publishing by arrangement with Fonthill Media LLC
For all general information, please contact Arcadia Publishing:
Telephone: 843-853-2070
Fax: 843-853-0044
E-mail: sales@arcadiapublishing.com
For customer service and orders:
Toll-Free 1-888-313-2665

www.arcadiapublishing.com

First published 2020

ISBN 978-1-63499-251-0

Typeset in 10.5pt on13pt Sabon
Printed and bound in England

ACKNOWLEDGMENTS

Special thanks to three people who played an integral role in creating this book: my husband, Bill; my mom, Bonnie Harper; and my dad, Roy Harper. Bill took photos, helped with research, and happily drove me wherever I needed to go. He was also the book's first reader and pointed out when I needed to clarify or try being succinct. Bonnie and Roy Harper have experienced firsthand much of Las Vegas's mid-twentieth-century history. Without their help, I might have missed some stories, sources, and events. Special thanks are also due to the many fine people at Fonthill Media.

CONTENTS

Acknowledgments   5

Introduction   9

1   On the Seedy Side   13

2   Wrong Place, Wrong Time   109

3   Unsolved   119

4   Casino Heists   126

5   Sorry, Not Sorry   136

6   Politicians   149

Epilogue   158

Bibliography   159

INTRODUCTION

Welcome to fabulous Las Vegas. Las Vegas (A.K.A. Sin City) is a magnet that draws seekers of fun from all over the world. Those who pack up and relocate here each year have plenty of company. Nearly every star who resides in Hollywood also has a home in Las Vegas. According to Vegas lore and a drop of historical fact, screen goddess Marilyn Monroe lived ever so briefly in Las Vegas. This was 1946, when she was still Norma Jean and it would be a while before stardom came to her. Years later, she would return as Marilyn, complete with blonde hair, tighter dresses, and heavier makeup. She would come to sit in the front row and cheer on Frank Sinatra and his pals (A.K.A. the Rat Pack,) when they entertained in the Copa Room at the Sands, the coolest place on the strip. A different time and already the mob had taken control.

Looking at the tangled freeways, the buildings, and bright lights of twenty-first-century Las Vegas, it is hard to imagine that this is a land that was inhabited thousands of years before the mob saw an advantage and moved in. Long before the first slot machine, the first entertainer, or the first divorcee came, the ancient people known as the Anasazi lived in this region. The Anasazi's disappearance and the reasons behind it may well be the first unsolved mystery of the Las Vegas area.

The Anasazi had long vanished from the region by the time Spanish missionaries came around in 1776, seeking a route between their missions in Arizona and those in California. Over time, this route (which covered parts of what would become modern-day Las Vegas) become known as Viejo Sendero or the Spanish Trail.

Fifty years after the missionaries, Spanish Mexican explorer Antonio Armijo set out with a party of traders on an expedition to find a trade route between New Mexico and Los Angeles. Seeking a shortcut, scout Rafael Rivera broke from the group and headed north. For his troubles,

Rivera was rewarded with a breathtaking sight of sun-dappled natural springs as far as the eye could see. Here was a respite from the hostile desert environment. Word quickly spread of the welcoming oasis. Before long, others would find their way to the natural springs. This area would become known as "Las Vegas," which is Spanish for the meadows. While mapping the region in 1844 explorer John C. Fremont, known as the Pathfinder, wrote:

> After a day's journey of 18 miles, in a northeasterly direction, we encamped in the midst of another very large basin, at a camping ground called Las Vegas a term which the Spaniards use to signify fertile or marshy plains, in contradistinction to llanos, which they apply to dry and sterile plains. Two narrow streams of clear water, four or five feet deep, gush suddenly with a quick current, from two singularly large springs; these, and other waters of the basin, pass out in a gap to the eastward. The taste of the water is good, but rather too warm to be agreeable; the temperature being 71 in the one and 73 in the other. They, however, afford a delightful bathing place.

Twenty years later, Nevada was admitted to the Union. It was 1864; Abraham Lincoln was up for re-election and the Civil War was raging. With Nevada's three electoral votes, Lincoln's victory was assured. The irony is that what we know as Las Vegas was in the Arizona Territory, at that time. It was not until two years later, in May 1866, that the present Nevada state boundary (that includes the present-day city of Las Vegas) was attained.

As far as major cities go, Las Vegas is new. It is the only major city to come into existence in the twentieth century. There is time, and then there is Las Vegas time, which moves at the speed of light; a Las Vegas hour is faster than a New York second. The new is continually morphing into the *passé*. Look around; there is nothing stagnant about this town, older buildings, and hotels are continually being remodeled and renamed. When space is needed for a bigger and more dazzling hotel and casino, the old one is promptly imploded. The ancient philosopher Heraclitus (530–470 B.C.) said that change is the only constant in life; Las Vegas wears those words as a badge of honor. Here is constant change and the city has built a reputation as a glamourous, free-and-easy metropolis in which excitement and alcohol can be had twenty-four hours a day. However, there is a downside.

Las Vegas's aura pulls in over 40 million tourists a year. The majority of them will go back home safely with memories and a phone full of selfies, yet some will not. Their fates will add to the city's crime statistics.

Las Vegas is a city with two tales to tell: the dazzling tale of never-seen-anything-like-it, where tourists walk the strip at all hours of the day and night intoxicated by booze and the excitement of it all; and there is the dark side, a sordid tale of a city founded by the greed of mobsters, a city enduring a high crime rate that has nothing to do with those same long-dead mobsters, and a city of clogged freeways and a cost of living that continually inches upward.

Everyone is looking to score—from the valet who parks your car, to the dealer who tosses you cards, the food server who serves your food, and the maid who changes your sheets. The score is a tip, expected by the valet, the dealer, the food server, and the maid—money, a gratuity, more commonly known as tokes in Las Vegas parlance, that you are expected to give. That is easy. Yet there is also the mugger, the junkie pickpocket, and the killer who hopes to score from some unsuspecting local or tourist. Those of us that know and love Las Vegas learned a long time ago that ours must be an unconditional love—exhilaration and anguish juxtaposed into our feelings for the quirky city that has no equal anywhere in the world, a city where anything can, and does, happen.

Crime happens everywhere, and Las Vegas is no exception. Vegas is a transient town, for all its newly created neighborhoods and infrastructure. People come and go. They are here for their own reasons. Some will find what they are looking for, put down roots, and stay. Others move on. In the meantime, crime happens. In Las Vegas, everyday ordinary crimes that involve everyday ordinary people can turn out to be the strangest crimes of all; such is the birthday murder of his wife by John Matthus Watson III, all so that she could not file for divorce and take advantage of California's community property laws—greed is what drove Watson.

Greed is one of the seven deadly sins and it is a common thread that weaves its way through many of the stories contained in this book. Love, jealousy, and hatred are emotions that play a big part in these stories as well. Perhaps the most unsettling stories are those that are completely senseless—those that involve people who happen to be in the wrong place at the wrong time, like the Route 91 Harvest Festival concert goers that found themselves in the scope of a madman's high-power rifles or the two young Las Vegas Police officers (Igor Soldo and Alyn Beck), who were sitting down to enjoy a pizza lunch before heading back out on the streets when their two killers rushed through the door and opened fire.

When a crime in Las Vegas involves a celebrity such as the unsolved murder of Tupac Shakur or the mysterious death of boxing great Sonny Liston, it is big news; so too is the murder that involves titillation. The 1998 death of legendary casino owner, Benny Binion's son Ted, is an example. Ted Binion's beautiful much younger girlfriend and her guy-on-the-side were accused and convicted of killing Binion for his money. In 2003, the Nevada Supreme Court overturned their convictions and the pair walked free. Binion was a long-time drug addict—a heroin user. While some mystery still surrounds his death, many believe he died of a drug overdose in the middle of his living room on Palomino Lane—intentional or not is the question.

Another case that is being discussed on the evening news magazine shows is the murder of seventy-one-year-old Thomas Burchard, a Salinas California psychiatrist, whose body was found in the trunk of a car belonging to a former Playboy model. The good doctor, it seems, had given Turner hundreds of thousands of dollars and been paying the blonde model's rent for quite some time. It also seems that she had a boyfriend on the side, and he was sharing her abode with her. This one has all the elements. Suspects Kelsey Nichole Turner and Jon Logan Kennison and their roommate Diana Pena have all been arrested. Turner and Kennison have pleaded not guilty. Pena claims to have the goods on them and is talking. However, at time of writing, the case has yet to be adjudicated.

I
ON THE SEEDY SIDE

Big Tipper at the Topless Cabaret

Carol Doda started it all in June 1964 when she dropped her top to become the first topless go-go dancer. It happened at the Condor Club in the north beach section of San Francisco. Doda was an immediate hit. As with all things that gain quick popularity, topless dancing was copied. Astute businessmen everywhere knew a good (and profitable) business model when they saw one. Soon, Sin City had its share of topless clubs, and while there have been some disputes, as well as some zoning and legal issues, topless entertainment is here to stay in Las Vegas.

It is a culture in which a young woman can make a lot of money fast, but she has to be clever and willing to compete. Other than reasonably good looks, and the ability to dance fairly well, not much else is required. Tokes make up most of a dancer's income and competition is stiff. A big tipper is coveted, and if she can, a dancer will keep a big tipper all to herself; this is not easy. Someone is always looking to turn a big tipper's eyes (and, of course, his cash) her way.

Alfonso "Slinky" Blake was a big tipper. This fact alone was enough to make him popular at the Olympic Garden Topless Cabaret. Everyone knows that the person who throws around cash always gets noticed by those who count on tokes as a large part of their income. Everyone also knows that the person, who makes a great show of their ability to toss around lots of cash, thrives on attention. Alfonso Blake was that guy. His favorite time to stop in at the topless club was around 2 a.m. The place was less crowded by then. Blake played the big shot, spending three or more hours drinking and visiting with the dancers and the cocktail waitresses. They knew him as Slinky, an R&B singer who had reached a point in his career where he had no money worries. Yet this was not the real Alfonso

Blake. In reality, he was a criminal with an extensive record—a bully who had three other dancers renting from him and they turned every dime they made over to him.

Slinky seemed friendly enough to Sophear Choy, who believed every word he told her. Convinced he truly was a kind and generous man, she introduced him to her sister, Kim Choy, and their friend, Priscilla Van Dine. The Choy sisters had recently come to Las Vegas from Southern California and, along with Priscilla Van Dine, were looking for an inexpensive apartment to rent. When they shared this information with Slinky, he had a solution: his large home had three extra bedrooms that he would rent to them for $500 a month each. That was cheap rent for a decent place to live in Las Vegas. Sophear was impressed, especially when he told her that he had so much money and truly liked helping others. He would even pay for their gym membership and health insurance. It might have seemed too good to be true to someone older and wiser, but not to nineteen-year-old Sophear. She thought of the money she could save and excitedly shared Slinky's offer with her sister and her friend. The three women talked it over and agreed that Slinky was offering them a good opportunity.

A deal was struck and the three young women began moving boxes of their belongings and furniture into Slinky's garage. A week passed. They still had not finished moving into Slinky's place when they learned about his house rules. The women were not allowed to have guests, they could not leave the house without him, and no one must know the location of his house. They quickly changed their minds. They would not be moving into Blake's place after all.

Kim called to tell him so. Gone was the caring man she thought she knew. The real Blake was furious that they had reneged on the deal. Still, he agreed to meet them at his house the next night so that they could come and get their stuff. The women arrived with a few friends that helped in the move. They had so much stuff it would not fit in their vehicles. They agreed to come back later that night and remove the rest of their belongings.

Sophear, Kim, and Priscilla were on the way back to his house when Blake called Sophear. Seething, he told her he was about to dump their stuff out on the street corner. "No! Don't do that," she begged. "Please don't do that!"

Yet as their vehicle neared his house, they saw that Slinky Blake had indeed dumped their belongings on the street corner. Kim brought the SUV to a sudden stop. While the women were loading boxes into their vehicle, two cars pulled up behind them; Blake leapt out and ran for Sophear. He angrily grabbed her around the neck and began slamming her against the boxes she had packed in the SUV. She fought back. The three women who had accompanied Blake surrounded her so that she could not run. Kim called 911, giving the operator their location.

Blake demanded, "Who you talkin' with?"

"My friend," Kim lied.

He slapped the phone from her hand.

"Kim! Help me up." Sophear cried, struggling to stand.

"What's wrong?" Kim asked her sister.

"I can't breathe ... I can't walk." Sophear cried.

"Okay, okay let's all calm down here." Blake said. "Help her walk!" He ordered Kim, then turning to his three women friends he said, "Go on now! I got this." When he was alone with Kim, Sophear, and Priscilla Blake, he said, "Okay. We're gonna take a little walk." Unsuspecting, they continued walking out into the desert with him, Sophear leaning on Kim for support.

Suddenly he stopped and said. "Look what Sophear made me do. She made me fucking stab her!" Kim gasped. This was the first time she noticed her sister's stab wounds. "This is far enough." Blake said, shoving Kim and Sophear. "Down on your knees!" He commanded them. Too scared to run, the women dropped to the ground. He slipped on a pair of gloves and pulled a gun from his pocket. "I warned you I didn't want any problems." He said.

Before they realized what was happening, he whirled around and shot Priscilla in the head twice, and then he turned the gun on Sophear, who clung to Kim. With Sophear and Priscilla dead, he took aim at Kim. Hysterical, she began screaming and waving her hands in front of her head. The first bullet ricocheted off the rings on her fingers. He took aim and shot her in the head, but Kim Choy would survive to tell detectives who had done this terrible thing to her, her sister, and their friend. She would recover and be able to give testimony that helped put Alfonso "Slinky" Blake behind bars.

The *coup de grâce* came in the testimony of the witness who overheard Blake, upon hearing that Kim survived: "That's impossible! I shot them all in the head twice." He cried. Nothing is impossible; surely the cold blooded killer realized exactly that when the jury found him guilty of two counts of first-degree murder for the deaths of Sophear Choy and Priscilla Van Dine and one count of attempted murder of Kim Choy with the use of a deadly weapon. On July 1, 2004, Blake was sentenced to two death sentences, and at time of writing, he awaits his appointment with the lethal injection chamber at the Ely State Prison in Ely Nevada.

Fred Willis—A Second Chance

> *A leopard cannot change its spots. One cannot change one's own nature.*
>
> *William Shakespeare*

The truth of those words, written centuries ago, would come back to haunt the Nevada parole board that set a monster free to kill again.

Back in the day, they worked in skimpy costumes designed to show as much skin as permissible, while hawking cigarettes, candy, and gum. These young women working as eye-candy were known as cigarette girls. Social mores change. With today's health-conscious society's disdain for smoking, such jobs have all but vanished in the U.S. Yet Las Vegas is not like other places, and you will still find cigarette girls at a few of the casinos along the Strip.

Twenty-five-year-old Bonnie Ann Woods worked as a cigarette girl and a cocktail waitress in a local casino when she encountered the man who would rape and murder her. There is no telling what promises he made Woods to get her from the casino where she worked to a room at the Motel 6 on Tropicana, but somehow, he gained her trust. She would pay for that trust with her life. Woods's body was discovered in the motel room on Friday morning just four days before Christmas 1984. When they apprehended him, Fred Willis confessed and pleaded no contest to second-degree murder and rape, thus sparing the taxpayer the expense of a trial. Due to this, he was sentenced to life in prison with the possibility of parole. Those three words—possibility of parole—meant hope that, one day, he might regain his freedom. During his incarceration, Willis did not waste his time in prison. He strategized.

He followed the rules, caused no problems, and did as he was told—an exemplary inmate you might say. This worked to his advantage when he appeared before the parole board in 1995 after having served eleven years in prison. Willis stated that given his good behavior he deserved a second chance. Prisons are notoriously overcrowded; easing those conditions is always a factor. The parole board wanted to believe. After all, the word "penitentiary" stems from penitent. Hopefully, Willis was rehabilitated and regretted the murder of Bonnie Ann Woods. Hopefully, there would not be any recidivism in Willis's future. The parole board agreed with him. If anyone deserved a second chance, it was Fred Willis; he could turn his life around and be a credit to society. He was therefore set free.

Yet Fred Willis was like that leopard; he could not change. In October 1997, two years after his release, the partially nude body of twenty-four-year-old Long Beach exotic dancer Zabrina Seaborn was discovered in a

Las Vegas alley. She had been raped, then strangled with the strap of her dress. After going through casino security videotape that showed Seaborn and a burly man at a Harrahs casino gaming table, police gathered enough evidence to arrest and charge Fred Willis with murder and rape.

When a trial date was set, Willis started thinking. A jury could well decide that he deserved the death penalty. He took a plea deal and pleaded guilty to first-degree murder. In the deal, the two rape charges were dropped, and so was the death penalty. A judge would determine whether or not he received life with the possibility of parole, or life without. Arguing for life without, the deputy district attorney said, "One life is too many, and two lives certainly are too many." The judge agreed, and Fred Willis was sentenced to life without the possibility of parole.

In a line that surely would have made Mark Twain proud, a writer for the *Las Vegas Review Journal* August 4, 1997, issue stated, "To his great credit, Willis didn't strangle a single woman when he was behind bars."

Another Second Chance Gone Wrong—Arthur Bomar

Members of the parole board are not fortune-tellers; they cannot see into the future. Surely, they believe that those they give a second chance to will come out and live productive law-abiding lives. Most of them do, but it does not always happen. Lest you go away thinking that Fred Willis is the only case of recidivism gone mad, consider the case of Arthur J. Bomar. On July 25, 1978, nineteen-year-old Bomar shot and killed Larry Carrier in Las Vegas during an argument over a parking space. He was paroled in 1990 after serving eleven years. While on parole in Nevada, Bomar petitioned for, and was granted, permission to relocate to Pennsylvania. That year, he was arrested for pulling a woman from her car and assaulting her. Nevada did not extradite him. Three years later, he was arrested for fighting in a bar. He had violated the terms of his parole. However, Nevada did not extradite him.

In 1996, the nude battered body of Aimee Willard was found in a parking lot. She had been raped and beaten to death with a tire iron. Bomar was arrested when his tire tracks matched those near the location and his DNA matched semen found on Aimee Willard's body. He was found guilty and sentenced to death in 1998. At time of writing, he is still on death row.

Murder at the Spy Shop

At twenty years old, Ginger Rios had her whole life ahead of her. A bride of five months, the dancer and backup singer for the Salsa Machine band was enjoying her new life. She and her husband had recently moved into a house with a lease option and she wanted to be a homeowner, but first, Ginger needed to clean up her credit. It was to be a quick stop. On April 4, 1997, with her husband waiting in the car, Ginger ran into the Spy Craft bookstore at 3507 Maryland Parkway to buy a book on improving credit. Fifteen minutes passed and she still had not come back to the car. Her husband glanced at her purse still sitting on the front passenger seat where she left it.

It did not take that long to buy a book, he reasoned. Growing impatient, he went looking for her. The shop owner told him she had bought a couple books and left. He went back to the car and waited. He went back and asked at the shop several more times only to receive the same answer; she bought a couple books and left the store. It was nearing 6 p.m.; Ginger had been gone two hours. The worried husband tried to ask again about her when the owner slammed the door in his face, angrily turning the open sign over to closed.

A month went by and there was still no sign of Ginger Rios. Her husband and her parents were frantic. Holding out hope, her parents clung to the idea that possibly, just possibly, she had left of her own volition. In desperation, the parents hired a local psychic, who assured them that Ginger was alive and would be found in the desert. Ginger's husband did not believe she had disappeared willingly. Like her parents, he did not know what to think. He had been outside in the car and never saw her come out the front door. Police were baffled as well. People disappear on their own all the time. If Ginger had met with foul play, the spouse would naturally be the first suspect. Then, too, suspicion fell on the store's owner, Craig Leslie Jacobsen (A.K.A. John Flowers), who denied knowing where Ginger was. He had surveillance cameras and videotape that could prove she had come and gone from the store. Yet, he explained, they had been reused and taped over. He would not agree to being interviewed by police.

Four months later, Jacobsen's wife, Cheryl Ciccone, got scared and talked. According to Ciccone, she was in the shop when Ginger Rios walked in. She had left on a quick five-minute errand. When she returned, Jacobsen was shaking and upset. At that moment, Rios's husband came into the store looking for her. Flowers explained that she had bought two books and walked out the front door. The husband left and they were alone in the shop again.

"Don't go in the back room," Jacobsen cautioned her. Ignoring him, Ciccone went to the back room where she discovered Ginger Rios's body in a puddle of blood. Jacobsen grabbed her around the throat, "I'll kill you and the baby if you tell anyone!"

"But why would you do this?" Ciccone asked.

"She tried to blackmail me." He answered. "I hit her in the nose and she just fell backwards and died." Jacobsen spent the rest of the day locked in the back room and wrapping Ginger Rios's body in plastic garbage bags. That night, they drove to Phoenix, Arizona. There, Jacobsen would buy cement to bury Rios in a shallow grave outside the city. Ciccone was able to lead detectives to the location where another woman's body was discovered nearby. While Rios's identity was quickly established, that of the other body was not. There were suspicions that Ginger Rios had been sexually assaulted after death; these were based on the fact that all of her jewelry was still in place with the exception of a genital piercing that was missing.

If Jacobsen had not pleaded guilty, he would have been charged with sexual assault and murder. After one reneged guilty plea, Jacobson entered a guilty but mentally unfit plea. He received a life sentence with the possibility of parole after twenty years. Before he completed those twenty years, Jacobsen was charged with the murder of Christina Marie Martinez and extradited to Arizona. There he would stand trial for the murder kidnapping of Martinez, whose body was discovered buried near Ginger Rios in the Arizona desert.

Cruelest of Them All

Brenda Stokes Wilson did something so horrific she did not want to think about it, but that was hours ago. She was jealous and she was angry. The thought that her fiancée was seeing another woman was driving her over the edge. What made it even worse was that the other woman happened to be her longtime friend Joyce Rhone, who was also a blackjack dealer at the Bellagio Hotel. Wilson had noticed the flirtation at a birthday party, and once she got the idea that her friend of seven years and her fiancée were friendlier to each other than was necessary, nothing could shake it.

The Bellagio has a strict policy that prohibits employees from coming onto the property on their days off. December 21, 2012—a Friday night— was Brenda Stokes Wilson's day off. She should not have been anywhere near the Bellagio, yet she was. She charged into the pit around 9.30 p.m. to where Rhone was dealing cards and leapt over the table. Before anyone realized what was happening, Wilson, a razor blade in each hand, began slicing at Rhone's face. The injured woman tried desperately to escape. She stumbled as Wilson pounced on her, razor blades flashing.

A quick-thinking patron jumped from the throng of stunned onlookers and shoved Wilson to the ground, holding her until security and police arrived. When she was taken in custody, Wilson said she would have killed Joyce Rhone if someone had not intervened. She was arrested and charged with burglary, battery with a deadly weapon, and mayhem with a deadly weapon.

While Wilson sat in jail one question remained—where was ten-year-old Jade Morris? Jade was the daughter of Wilson's boyfriend; the little girl was last seen around 5 p.m. when Wilson took her out to go Christmas shopping on December 21. Family would later say that there was nothing unusual in this. Wilson and Jade were fond of each other; they often went shopping together. While volunteers searched for Jade, police questioned Wilson on the whereabouts of the child, but she steadfastly refused to answer any of their questions. While executing a search warrant on her apartment and vehicle, they discovered bloody clothing in the apartment and blood in her car. They were sure they knew what happened to Jade Morris if only they could find her.

The little girl's body was found six days later when a man walking his dog made a grisly discovery. Identification came through dental records and facial recognition; there was no question that the child's death was a homicide. She had died of multiple stab wounds.

Charged with the death of Jade Morris, Wilson pleaded not guilty until she realized that the prosecution intended to seek the death penalty. The murder of a child is incomprehensible. Chances were good that she would be found guilty of killing Jade. If that were the case, she would end up in Nevada's execution chamber. She quickly agreed to plead guilty in order to avoid the death penalty. She was sentenced to life in prison without the possibility of parole.

In sentencing her, Clark County District Court Judge Kathleen Delaney said, "Jade lives on the way she does in the memories of people who loved her and cared for her. All we can do today is find the justice in the outcome of the sentence."

O. J. Simpson's Memorabilia Madness

Room 1203 in the courtyard complex of the Palace Hotel Casino was the scene of the crime. Not quite as nice as the tower rooms, the rooms in the courtyard offered quicker access to the swimming pool. Yet do not waste your time looking for the room or the courtyard complex as it is no longer there. In true Vegas fashion, the Palace has since demolished, upgraded, and remodeled the area.

On October 3, 1995, O. J. Simpson was acquitted for the murders of his ex-wife Nicole Brown Simpson and Ron Goldman. He would not be so lucky in the 1997 civil suit brought against him by the victims' families. In that suit, Simpson was found liable for the deaths and the plaintiffs were awarded $33.5 million in damages. If that was not enough for Simpson to pay, the judgment was renewed in court two years later. The sum he owed was now $58 million. No matter what he did, Simpson would be tied to that debt for the rest of his life and beyond.

Simpson's new problems with the law started because he was angry. Approximately 42 million people visit Las Vegas each year. On September 13, 2007, O. J. Simpson was one of them. He had come to Las Vegas for a wedding. While there, a friend informed him that a certain memorabilia dealer was selling a lot of his stuff. This stuff, claimed Simpson, had been stolen from him and he wanted it back. Simpson and a group of friends devised a plan. One of them rented room 1203 at the Palace and invited the dealer to bring some of his merchandise for a client to take a look at.

Simpson and his cohorts showed up at room 1203, armed and ready to get his stuff back one way or the other. They charged into the room and demanded the stolen stuff. The shocked dealer denied that the memorabilia was stolen. Simpson loudly insisted it was, as he and his accomplices began scooping stuff up and stuffing it in pillowcases. When the dealer balked, he was threatened with a gun by one of the men with Simpson. What Simpson did not know was that one of his accomplices had set up an audio recorder to record all the action.

On that device Simpson was heard saying, "Don't let nobody out of this room.... Motherfucker, you think you can steal my shit and sell it?" This statement was a big mistake on Simpson's part. It would result in a kidnapping charge against him. Eleven other charges were brought against O. J. Simpson, including conspiracy to commit a crime and burglary while in possession of a deadly weapon.

On December 5, 2008, snow was piled 2 feet high in other parts of the country. Yet in Las Vegas, at the tip of the Mojave Desert, it was just another sunny day. By 7 a.m., a crowd started gathering outside the Clark County Regional Justice Center. Some held up signs that read "Free O. J." Whatever happened, it would be newsworthy; it always was with former football legend O. J. and it had been so ever since the day a cameraman in a helicopter focused in on the white Bronco as it sped down the freeway with police cars in pursuit. A star had fallen. Perverse it may be, but fallen stars are hot news.

People waited outside courtroom 15A to see whether or not they would win the raffle for one of the coveted fifteen seats assigned for the public's use. Two months earlier and exactly thirteen years to the day of his acquittal for the murder of ex-wife Nicole Brown and Ron Goldman, Simpson had been found guilty of all ten charges against him. On this day, he was set to be sentenced and most of the available seats had been given to news media and those connected with the case.

With tough cookie the honorable Jackie Glass presiding, no one expected Simpson to receive a short slap on the wrist stay at one of Nevada's prisons. Still, the aging O. J. may have hoped. Two of those lucky enough to win a ticket were Fred and Kim Goldman, father and sister of Ron Goldman, the young man who was brutally murdered alongside Simpson's estranged wife, Nicole. Also in attendance were Denise Brown, Nicole Simpson's sister, and. O. J.'s oldest daughter, his sister, and his brother-in-law.

Clearly the years had taken their toll. O. J. Simpson, in jail garb and shackled, was far different from the handsome football hall of famer who had vaulted through airports hawking Hertz rental cars in television commercials *c.* 1970. Gone was the smiling defendant, declared not guilty of the 1995 brutal double murder that stunned the world. On this morning, Simpson appeared to be a broken old man. He seemed to be fighting back tears when he addressed the judge.

> Your Honor, I stand before you today sorry. Somewhat confused. I feel like apologizing to the people of the state of Nevada. I've been coming to Nevada since 1959. I worked summer jobs for my uncle in '60 and '61, and I've been coming ever since, and I've never gotten into any trouble. People have always been fine to me.
>
> When I came here, I came for a wedding. I didn't come here to ... I didn't come here to reclaim property. I was told it was here. When he told me that Monday, that stuff was in Nevada when he heard nobody was going to be in Nevada, I called my kids. I talked to my sisters, I called the Brown family and I told them I had a chance to get some of our property, property that over the years we've seen being sold on the Internet. We've seen pictures of ours that were stolen from our home going into the tabloids.
>
> We've called the police and ask them what to do. They've told us what to try to do, but you can never find out who was selling it, and this was the first time I had an opportunity to catch the guys red handed who had been stealing from my family. In no way did I mean to hurt anybody, to steal anything from anybody. I just wanted my personal things.

Judge Glass was nobody's fool. Known for handing down long sentences, Judge Glass was not buying it. "When you take a gun with you and you take men with you in a show of force, that is not just a 'Hey, give me my stuff back.' That's something else and that's what happened here," she admonished him.

Everyone in this courtroom today was probably thinking about that other trial in Los Angeles, the one everyone thought was a slam dunk—

when a years younger O. J. Simpson stood trial for the murder of his ex-wife Nicole Brown Simpson and her friend Ron Goldman. It was the trial of the century, and on October 3, 1995, Simpson was found not guilty; the glove did not fit, so the jury had to acquit.

Judge Glass was certainly mindful of that other trial. Before imposing sentence on the former football star, she told those in the courtroom, "I'm not here to try and cause any retribution or any payback for anything else I want that to be perfectly clear to everyone."

She then sentenced Simpson to thirty-three years in prison with parole eligibility after nine years. He was granted parole in July 2017. He has been released from Nevada's Lovelock prison and is reportedly living the good life in Las Vegas. It was very close to the twenty-fifth anniversary of the Nicole Simpson and Ron Goldman murder when Simpson launched his own Twitter account. He does not lack for followers and seems to have plenty to say.

While O. J. tweets, the Las Vegas hospitality industry remains ever vigilant of guest safety. The incident that put Simpson in prison is probably one reason that every Vegas hotel and casino implemented new rules. No one, not even hotel guests, is allowed to hop on hotel elevators without first presenting I.D. or a room keycard.

I Will Do It Myself—Scott Dozier

> It would perhaps be nice to be alternatively the victim and the
> executioner.
>
> Charles Baudelaire

Jeremiah Miller was twenty-two years old and he wanted wealth. He saw a quick route to this by grabbing a piece of the drug pie. In his quest for ephedrine, a necessary component of methamphetamine, he met Scott Dozier in Phoenix. "No problem," Dozier assured him; he would gladly help him buy some, if he met him in Las Vegas. Eager to begin production of methamphetamine, Jeremiah Miller went to Las Vegas. However, the deal fell through—there was no ephedrine and Miller went back to Phoenix empty-handed.

A few weeks later, he received a phone call from Dozier. A dealer had been located. If Miller would come back to Vegas, they could make a deal. Jeremiah Miller borrowed $12,000 and drove to Las Vegas. There, he was to meet Dozier at the La Concha motel on the strip.

On April 18, 2002, as he pulled into the parking lot, Miller probably did not know that the La Concha lobby was designed by prominent African

American architect Paul Revere Williams, whose projects included the First Church of Christ Scientist (Lear Theater) in Reno, the Shrine Auditorium in Los Angeles, and the Beverly Hills homes of countless movie stars. Nor did he know that during its heyday, the motel had welcomed celebrities such as Flip Wilson, Muhammad Ali, and Ronald Reagan. The La Concha had seen better days and they were long gone. Yet the most important thing Jeremiah Miller did not know that afternoon was just how dangerous and evil his friend, Scott Dozier, truly was.

Miller quickly parked, slid out of the car, and scanned the motel. Dozier's room was easy enough to find. He knocked on the door. Dozier opened it just wide enough for Miller to squeeze into the room. That was the last time anyone would see Jeremiah Miller alive. Once he was inside the room, Dozier shot and killed the young man, who was fluent in Spanish and had volunteered for Habitat for Humanity. Dozier did not care about any of that. All he had wanted was more drug money and Miller had cash. Like any predator, he had quickly realized that Jerimiah Miller (drug dealer or not) was naïve—just someone to be taken advantage of and cruelly done away with. He had killed the year before—in Phoenix—and gotten away with. He would dispose of Miller's body the same way, pulling the bleeding body into the bathroom and placing it in the bathtub. There he would saw it into pieces and stuff most of them in a suitcase that he left near an apartment complex on the other side of town.

Nearly a week went by and Miller's parents were concerned. It was not like their son not to check in with them. A missing person report was filed. With still no sign of Jerimiah, the frantic parents called Dozier's room at the La Concha. Had he seen Jerimiah? He calmly informed them that Jeremiah had left with a woman and he had not seen him since. On April 25, a maintenance man at the Copper Sands Apartments noticed a horrible smelling suitcase in the dumpster. With the help of a co-worker, he lifted the suitcase out of the dumpster. The dismembered body was missing its head and part of its arms and legs. Identification of the body was determined through tattoos on the shoulder. Jeremiah Miller had been found.

Now detectives wanted to know who killed him. They would get their answer when a former friend of Dozier's came forward to tell them about helping him hide the torso of Jason Green in the Arizona desert a year earlier. Detectives went to the location in the desert and soon located the dismembered body of Green. Things were unraveling for Scott Dozier.

Another person told Las Vegas detectives about the day that Dozier asked him for a bucket of concrete. This did not seem strange to him because Dozier sometimes worked at the La Concha as a maintenance man. This, detectives believed, was how Dozier had hidden Jerimiah Miller's head. The head and legs were never found.

Arizona sentenced Scott Dozier to twenty-two years for the murder of Jason Green. The state then extradited him to Nevada to stand trial for the murder of Jerimiah Miller. Wanting justice for their son, Miller's parents attended every day of Dozier's trial. The prosecution brought in a witness who took the stand to testify that Scott Dozier had told her that he shot Jeremiah Miller in the back of the head. On September 25, 2007, Dozier was convicted of first-degree murder in the death of Jeremiah Miller. Nine days later, he was given the death sentence for the murder.

He would spend eleven years on Nevada's death row. In that time, the death sentence was appealed to the Nevada State Supreme Court, which upheld it on January 23, 2012. Dozier's final execution date was set for July 2018. However, Alvogen, the drug company that manufactured the sedative to be used in the execution, sued the state of Nevada over the state's intended use of its drug. The execution was halted and the debate started—which drugs insured a humane a painless death for the lethal injection? Dozier was not stupid. He realized he was never walking out of prison a free man. He just wanted to be done with it. He claimed that he did not want to die, but the waiting was unbearable. If he would eventually end up in the state of Nevada's execution chamber, why wait? So he sued the state of Nevada to speed things along.

The fight was still going on when Dozier took matters into his own hands and hanged himself in his cell at the Ely State Penitentiary on January 5, 2019, thus making his execution a do-it-yourself event.

Deadly Love

> *Let us go then, you and I/When the evening is spread out against the sky.*
>
> "The Love Song of J. Alfred Prufrock," T. S. Eliot

Adrian Grodnick and Betty Baron came to Las Vegas to be married. Before that happened, something snapped, destroying the lovebirds' plans.

On September 13, 1952, Bugsy Siegel was dead and most likely forgotten. However, business is business; his snazzy penthouse suite at the Fabulous Flamingo was available and being rented out on a nightly basis. Grodnick wanted nothing but the best for his bride. He and Baron checked into the plush $35-a-night suite and prepared to enjoy their stay. That certainly would not rent much of a room today, but back in 1952, it was enough to rent a very nice place. In today's cash, it would be about $331, which the soon-to-be groom could well afford.

Nineteen-year-old Adrian was the son of a wealthy New York businessman. He and Betty, twenty-six, met when he came to Los Angeles and rented an apartment in a building her parents managed. She was a recent graduate of UCLA and he was soon to be inducted into the army. They fell in love and were making plans for their future, which included marriage and children. Like many young couples, they were in a hurry, and after talking it over, they gave up Betty's dream of a big wedding, opting instead for a quick Las Vegas wedding. Since money was not a problem, Adrian had rented a car and they drove to Vegas for the weekend.

Did Adrian Grodnick plan the murder–suicide all along, or did something happen during those two days that pushed him over the edge? Investigators were later able to determine that sometime during their stay, Adrian Grodnick went to a nearby pawnshop and purchased a gun. Also, on the night of September 15, 1952, in Benjamin Bugsy Siegel's former penthouse suite, Adrian Grodnick put two bullets in the brain of the woman he loved. The long-dead gangster was not telling any tales. Neither was the pretty brunette murder victim, or the young man who shot her. After killing his fiancée, the young Adrian Grodnick turned the gun on himself.

Several hours later, two housekeepers knocked on the door. Following no answer, they knocked again and again. They finally forced their way into the suite. Sprawled across the bed were the nude bodies of a man and woman. They would not need room service, fresh towels, or turn-down service again ever.

Back in the monochrome television days of *Dragnet* and Sgt. Joe Friday, murder happened but seldom in a lavish hotel penthouse. The more they discovered, the more detectives were puzzled. Money was not the motive, it had to be love, or lack thereof. There was a myriad of theories. Perhaps Adrian Grodnick was so frightened of the military that he killed Betty and himself; although this does not make a lot of sense, little about murder–suicide does. Yet another theory put forth had Grodnick apprehensive about his sexual prowess. Was the worldly Betty wiser in that regard? Did it matter? Maybe he was insanely jealous. Maybe there were accusations, tears, and threats to end the romance. No one will ever know why Adrian Grodnick chose to kill his fiancée and himself in Bugsy Siegel's old digs.

The Roxie Club Scandal

There will be no legalized prostitution in Clark County if I can prevent it.

Clark County Commission Chairman Ira Earl, 1946

There is no pun intended, but legal prostitution in Nevada is tricky. Of Nevada's sixteen counties, six do not permit brothels (legalized prostitution.) These are Clark (where Las Vegas is situated), Washoe, Douglas, Lincoln, Pershing, and Eureka. The state's capital, Carson City (an independent city), also bans brothels.

Located in Nye County, Pahrump is 63 miles from Las Vegas. Pahrump offers the closest legal prostitution to Las Vegas. On October 16, 2018, Dennis Hof, the flamboyant owner of the Love Ranch in Pahrump, was found dead in his bedroom here. Foul play was not suspected. The seventy-two-year-old Hof lived the high life. Besides that, he was overweight, and a diabetic. He had also spent the previous night partying in celebration of his birthday. The coroner said it was a heart attack; marijuana and sildenafil were also found in Hof's system. Sildenafil is a generic name for the active ingredient in erectile dysfunction medication like Viagra and Revatio. Hof was a trailblazer as far as adult entertainment goes. He was also a newly minted politician. At the time of his death, he was running for state assemblyman for District 36. He might have appreciated the irony of having been the first owner to have died in his own whorehouse. Hof also claimed another first by being the first person in Nevada history to win an election posthumously.

A century before Dennis Hof celebrated his final birthday, prostitution was enjoying its early, carefree years. In those early days (1905–1910), Las Vegas did not have a problem with prostitution. As long as it was kept in one area of town, the law did not concern itself. This area was known as Block 16 and it was situated near the railroad station. The Honolulu, the Red Front, the Jazz, the Double O, and the Arizona were some of the colorful places in Block 16 that offered prostitutes. The rest of Las Vegas would be safe from the vice that went on here. Las Vegas Sheriff Sam Gay had a *laissez-faire* attitude regarding prostitution. He had a favorite saying: "If you're not bothering people, go about your business."

The area flourished even during the thirteen years (1920–1933) that the Volstead Act made prohibition the law of the land. Undeterred with what Washington, D.C., mandated, the saloons in Block 16 continued to sell alcohol. This all changed in 1941 when the army built the Air Corp. Gunnery School (Nellis Air Force Base) on the north end of the Las Vegas Valley.

The government wanted all brothels near military bases closed down. The Gunnery School was not that far from Block 16 with its prostitution and the military did not like this. Block 16 was not an area that servicemen should be visiting, but they were. Las Vegas was offered an ultimatum—get rid of Block 16 or the city would be off limits to servicemen. In 1942, Block 16 was closed down.

In 1946, the war was over and prostitution had relocated 4 miles out of town to an area known as Formyle on the Boulder Highway. The brothel at Formyle was Roxie's, owned by former Los Angeles cop Eddie Clippinger and his wife, Roxie. They believed themselves smarter than the others. When an occasional patron had too much excitement and died on the premises, his body was found elsewhere, thus preventing any problems for Roxie's. The corpse also had an empty wallet and all his jewelry was missing, but the Clippingers had connections in the form of payouts to Sheriff Glen Jones, which meant they operated their establishment hassle free. As it turned out, they were not the only owners of Roxie's. Newspaperman Hank Greenspan got the goods on the whole operation that bribed politicians, bugged rooms, and bribed customers.

Eddie Clippinger was from Los Angeles. While working for the LAPD vice squad, Clippinger certainly would have known Guy McAfee, who was head of the department at the same time. During his time as head of the vice squad, McAfee owned brothels and gambling clubs. One just has to wonder how much Eddie Clippinger learned about such illegal activities from his boss, Guy McAfee. Like McAfee, Eddie Clippinger maintained his California residence.

He was running a brothel on D Street in the red-light district of San Bernardino California in early 1940s. Authorities were looking the other way and money was being made; then, residents demanded the city clean up its infamous D Street, and the FBI joined forces with local law enforcement to see that it was done. Eddie Clippinger decided it might be a good time to take his business savvy to Las Vegas. He would run the brothel at the Meadows on Boulder Highway. The brothel was short-lived thanks to residents in the area who did not want a brothel so close to their neighborhood. Like the people in San Bernardino, they demanded that city officials close the brothel down. All was not lost, however. The very married Eddie met a cute prostitute by the name of Roxie and fell madly in love. The wife was history in his eyes. With the divorce finalized, he and Roxie wed and went into business together.

Eddie and Roxie Clippinger were facing federal charges and anxious to unload the brothel. In an amazing show of naiveté, Roxie opened her books to a man posing as a prospective buyer. Little did she know that the conversations were recorded and would come back to bite both her and

Eddie where it hurt. If she was shocked, so was Sheriff Glen Jones, who talked about what his payouts might be and boasted about his connections. Jones was not the only politician to get caught in the scandal. Nevada Lieutenant Governor Clifford Jones was also swept up. As co-owner of the mob hotel The Thunderbird, Jones (no relation to Glen Jones) was subpoenaed to the Kefauver hearing investigating mob connections in Las Vegas.

During their trial, Eddie Clippinger claimed to be a real estate broker. In July 1954, both Clippingers were convicted of conspiracy to violate the White Slave Traffic act. Eddie Clippinger was sentenced to three years at the federal prison at McNeil Island in Washington. The infamous Robert Stroud (Birdman of Alcatraz) spent some time at McNeil in the 1920s for having killed a bartender. While at McNeil, Stroud killed a guard. Other inmates who had spent some time at McNeil were Charles Manson and Alvin (Creepy) Karpis.

Roxie wept as Eddie was led from the courtroom. While he went to Washington, Roxie was sent to the women's prison in Alderson, West Virginia. Fifty years after Roxie's residency at Alderson, the diva of decorating and cooking, Martha Stewart, was incarcerated there. During Stewart's stay, the prison was referred to as Camp Cupcake.

Roxie spent her three years at Alderson and like Eddie was paroled to Southern California (where the Clippingers actually lived). Their business in Nevada was concluded; they would never return to Las Vegas as to do so would have been a parole violation.

On November 21, 1953, with Eddie Clippinger safely tucked away at McNeil Island, two men decided that now might be a good time to rob the brothel. With their faces covered by masks, the robbers pushed their way into Roxie's, waving pistols and yelling threats. Their take was $150 in silver dollars and thousands of dollars in paper money. They got away in what was described as a "shiny car" and were never caught.

Sheriff Butch Leypoldt and newly elected Clark County District Attorney George Dickerson wanted Roxie's closed. They were well-aware that through his three terms, Sheriff Jones had become enmeshed with the brothel's scandals. In April 1954, federal agents raided Roxie's and closed it down permanently. It may have been the end of an era, but it was not the end of legalized prostitution in the state of Nevada.

Guy McAfee—The Man Who Named the Strip

Las Vegas's Strip might have been called something altogether different if not for the 1938 ousting of Los Angeles Mayor Frank L. Shaw. The crooked mayor's downfall began with the 1937 bombing of a private investigator, who was investigating corruption within Shaw's administration. Yet it was the subsequent indictment and conviction of LAPD Captain Earl Kynette for the bombing attack that spelled doom for Shaw's mayoral career. The following year, voters kicked Shaw out of office. Thus he became the first mayor of a major city to be recalled from office. His administration is still seen as the most corrupt in the city's history.

Judge Fletcher Bowron was elected to replace Shaw, vowing to get rid of corruption and lawlessness, which included prostitution, illegal gambling, and narcotics. Suddenly, things were too hot for former vice cop Guy McAfee, who had discovered that there was more money to be made in illegal gambling than there was in being a cop.

Bowron had barely begun his cleanup of corruption when McAfee and his wife, screen actress June Brewster, moved to Las Vegas. Nevada's legalized gambling was a chance for criminals in other parts of the country to make a fresh start—legally. In Las Vegas, McAfee bought the Pair-O-Dice Club, the first nightclub on Arrowhead Highway (Highway 91). In 1942, he sold the Pair-O-Dice, took the money, and bought interest in other downtown casinos. Three years later, he bought the Golden Nugget Casino in a $1 million deal—not a bad chunk of change for a former cop, especially during a time when World War II raged.

Although McAfee bid Los Angeles goodbye as far as business went, he and his wife maintained a posh residence in Beverly Hills. In honor of Hollywood's Sunset Strip, he started calling that section of Arrowhead Highway where his casinos were located "the Strip." That might have been a long time ago in Vegas years, but the name stuck.

At some point, McAfee certainly renewed his acquaintance with brothel owner, Eddie Clippinger, who had worked under him at the LAPD vice squad. McAfee is rumored to have had his hand in many pots, and records show that he took a $25,000 dollar cut of the Clippingers' prostitution racket at least once from their petty cash.

Goodsprings—The Death of Paul Coski

Goodsprings is 40 miles southwest of Las Vegas down I-15. With a population of not much more than 200 people give or take, if there are any similarities between the two, it would be the tenuous connection with film stars and gambling-related crime.

In 1942, screen star Clark Gable spent a harrowing night at the Pioneer Saloon in Goodsprings while awaiting word of his wife actress Carole Lombard, whose plane had crashed at nearby Mt. Potosi. The news, when he finally heard it, was not good. All twenty-two people aboard flight three had perished in the fiery crash. Lombard's death is the biggest news story in Goodsprings's history.

Jane Alice Peters (Carole Lombard) was a seven-year-old girl in faraway Fort Wayne, Indiana, the day Paul Coski's luck turned cold. It was late in the morning of June 26, 1915. Summer's ungodly heat had given way to a gentle breeze that wafted through the Pioneer Saloon. Daylight would come in a few hours and with it the heat.

Unaware of time or temperature, six men played stud poker in a corner of the Pioneer Saloon. Twenty-seven-year-old Paul Coski, Joe Armstrong, Roy Blood, Tom Lowe, and F. J. Schroeder were so intent on the cards they did not notice the bartender who hovered nearby. When it came time for Coski to deal, Blood, Armstrong, and Schroeder folded. Rather than leave the saloon, they watched as Coski and Lowe continued their card game.

"You dealt yourself a card from the bottom," Armstrong told Coski. "You and Tom should split the pot and be done with it." The bartender agreed with Armstrong—Coski had cheated. The pot, they said, should be divided and the game ended. However, card sharp Paul Coski did not want to do that. He angrily grabbed for the money. Armstrong leapt up and pushed him back. "There's no call for cheating."

Coski tried to leap over the table. The smaller and older Armstrong pulled his gun. Coski grabbed his wrist to disarm him. Armstrong fired, hitting Coski in the hand. Coski lunged for Armstrong, who fired another shot. Paul Coski fell to the floor dead.

When notified of the shooting, Clark County Sheriff Gay, district attorney Henderson, and coroner Harkins drove out to the Pioneer Saloon. They arrived around 5 a.m., and an investigation and inquest were held. No one had liked Paul Coski. He was not a victim one could feel much sympathy for. He had a reputation as being violent and hard to get along with, especially when he had been drinking, which he had been doing on that night. No one had a good word to say about the cheating miner. Armstrong, on the other hand, was well-liked. He had never given anyone a day's trouble. Following a verdict of self-defense, Armstrong was exonerated. A death certificate was filled out and Coski's body was wrapped in sheets, placed in a pine box, and buried in the Goodsprings cemetery. The bullet holes remain in the wall of the Pioneer Saloon to this day, a reminder of the consequences of cheating at cards and getting caught.

A copy of coroner Harkins's letter hangs on the wall. It is obvious that the coroner knew what Coski was all about: "He could whip any two men in or around Goodsprings and made a practice of doing the same once in a while when he would get to drinking. When he was sober, he was a gentleman."

Of the shooter Armstrong, the newspaper said, "At the time of the Custer massacre, Armstrong was a scout attached to the command of General Terry and was among the first to arrive at the scene of carnage two days after the terrible slaughter."

Overton Bank Robbery

Betty Willis was born in Overton on May 20, 1923. She was the graphic designer responsible for the famous "Welcome to Fabulous Las Vegas" sign and she was born in Overton, which is about 63 miles northeast of Las Vegas. Not everything in the Las Vegas area is new, neon, and glass. Overton is near the site of Nevada's lost city, Pueblo Grande de Nevada, where ancient people lived from approximately 8000 BC.

Overton is small compared to Las Vegas. A little over 4,200 people live here. Fewer people lived here in 1967. Among them was the Conger family. When he was paroled from the Federal Correctional Institute in Lompoc, California, twenty-three-year-old Terry Lynn Conger came to Overton to be with his family. His parents welcomed him into their home in the hope that he would straighten out his life and make something of himself. He took a job as a construction worker and convinced them that he was trying to turn his life around. He was not.

While Las Vegas was seeing an uptick in its crime statistics, Overton remained a safe little haven where crime seldom occurred. This changed on August 29, 1967. Shortly before its 3 p.m. closing time, Terry Lynn Conger walked into the Bank of Las Vegas (Overton Branch). He herded the bank manager and the two tellers into the vault where he shot each of them in the head. According to detectives, Conger then callously stacked their bodies "like cordwood," and made away with $35,000. He would not be on the run long. Las Vegas police and the FBI swarmed Overton. Two and a half hours after the robbery and the murders, Conger was captured at a nearby ranch.

In September 1968, Conger was found guilty of the murders and the bank robbery and sentenced to life without the possibility of parole. In June 1973, he appealed his conviction in the Nevada Supreme Court, claiming that he only pleaded guilty to the three counts of murder because he had been promised that the federal charge of bank robbery would be dropped if he did so. The court found against him. He died in prison on September 19, 1999.

A Money-Hungry Ghost Forced Him to Kill

On December 13, 2001, Samuel Marquez desperately needed money. He intended to rob and kill bartender Richard Adamicki from the moment he walked through the door of the Lake Mead Tavern. It was barely past midnight and the bar was almost empty. Marquez drank a couple of beers and played a few hands of video poker then tried to get money from the ATM using his credit card. By that time, it was just him and the bartender. Marquez went outside and got a bat that he hid in his pants. Being careful that Adamicki would not notice the weapon, he stepped over to the ATM and pulled the bat out. Carefully hiding the bat between the ATM machine and the jukebox, Marquez tried to get money from the ATM several more times. Adamicki tried to help him with the machine, and then took his place at the end of the bar. He had a newspaper to read.

Marquez grabbed the bat. Before Adamicki realized what was happening, Marquez swung the bat, hitting him in the head and knocking him to the floor. With his victim down, Marquez drew the bat back and struck him with it again and again. He then ransacked the cash register, taking $2,700. As he was leaving, he bent and pulled Adamicki's wallet from his pocket.

It is said that criminals are stupid, and there is probably a lot of truth to that statement. Marquez, who lived very close to the Lake Mead Tavern, was arrested within a day, done in by ATM receipts and video cameras. He confessed. Richard Adamicki was alive in the ICU unit of a local hospital. The luckless bartender would remain on life support for two months before succumbing to the terrible injuries Marquez had inflicted on him; the charges against Marquez were therefore upped to murder. Marquez told detectives that he remembered doing crystal meth, drinking alcohol, and smoking marijuana on the night of the murder, but he did not remember the actual murder. It did not matter what he remembered as the video cameras told the story.

During the trial, the defense presented a forensic psychologist, who told the court that Marquez had a paranoid schizophrenic psychosis that led him to believe a woman ghost from El Salvador followed him about ordering him to do things. The ghost had wanted the money from the cash register and so ordered Marquez to take it. He feared she would kill him if he did not obey her. You have got to wonder what on earth a ghost could possibly want with money. Whatever the reason, according to Marquez, this ghost wanted money and she was the reason for the robbery and the killing.

Marquez was convicted and sentenced to 100 years. He appealed to the Nevada Supreme Court using his belief in ghosts as evidence of insanity. The Supreme Court disagreed, rejecting the appeal in a two–one decision.

The Krupp Diamond Heist

The scene of the crime is the ranch house, which serves as the visitors' center, at the Spring Mountain State Park. This pastoral setting belies the fact that here in 1959, one of the biggest diamond heists in the state of Nevada took place.

Beautiful German actress Vera Hossenfeld liked marriage. When one did not work out, there was always divorce, and then another marriage. German war criminal industrialist Alfried Krupp became Vera's fourth and last husband on May 19, 1952. He was also the wealthiest. They married shortly after his release from Landsberg Prison. Three years later, in 1955, he purchased the 520-acre Bar Nothing Ranch at the base of the Wilson Cliffs for Vera. The price was $1 million, which is roughly equivalent to $9.5 million today.

The ranch had gone through several owners and a few name changes since James B. Wilson and his partner George Anderson filed a claim on it in 1876, calling it the Sand Stone Ranch. Vera had her own ideas. The first thing she did was to rename the ranch the Spring Mountain Ranch. Vera had come to love the desert with its western lifestyle. Although she knew nothing about ranching, she dug her cowboy boots in and was determined to learn. She took classes on animal husbandry and ranching and was eventually accepted by other ranchers.

She would live at the ranch longer than any other owner, and with the exception of Howard Hughes, Vera was also the ranch's wealthiest owner. Once she settled into Las Vegas and ranch life, Vera wanted her freedom from Alfried, who, as a convicted war criminal, was barred from entering the U.S. She was lonely. He was in Germany and could not come to her. Six months before she sued him for a divorce and millions, Alfried Krupp gifted Vera with a stunning 33.6-carat Asscher-cut diamond ring he had purchased from world-renowned jeweler Harry Winston. She loved the ring, but not him. She bid him *auf wiedersehen*; this may have been where the so-called curse of Krupp Diamond began. After all, it certainly was not very lucky for Alfried, who may have hoped such an ostentatious diamond might keep him forever in Vera's heart. The type IIa diamond was the rarest natural diamond, free from all impurities, containing very little nitrogen, and was nearly colorless—quite a gift, but not enough to keep Vera.

The curse must have ended with Alfried because the diamond proved lucky for Vera Krupp. She got the money, the ranch, and the diamond. Unlike some who keep their jewelry safely hidden away, Vera wore the ring wherever she went. Incongruous as it may have been, she wore the sizeable sparkler along with her standard ranch gear of jeans, western shirt, and boots.

Big diamonds get noticed, and Vera's caught the eye of a small-time crook by the name of George Reves. Most people would probably assume such a hefty stone was a fake—not Reves. He knew diamonds, and he realized the rock was real and worth a lot of money ($275,000 dollars to be exact, which in today's money is well over $2 million). Reves got a crew together and made a plan to steal the diamond.

On April 11, 1959, Vera and her foreman were relaxing after dinner with drinks in front of the stone fireplace. Their *tête-à-tête* was interrupted by a loud knock at the door. Thinking it was the blacktop crew, Vera opened the door. She was shoved aside by Reves as he and his men pushed their way into the house. Reves held Vera and the foreman at gunpoint while his accomplices tied them up, back to back. Grabbing Vera's hand, Reves tore the prized diamond from her finger, yanking it so hard he drew blood. This is what the thieves had come for; nonetheless, they ransacked the house and stole other pieces of jewelry, a gun, and approximately $7,000 in cash.

Believing that the stolen diamond would be transported across state lines, the F.B.I. quickly got involved. Within six weeks, the case was solved. The diamond and Reves were found in Elizabeth, New Jersey; Reves and his crew went to prison and the diamond was returned to Vera.

Vowing to never again be a victim, Vera had a secret bedroom and passageway built in the ranch house. To get into the room, someone would have to go through her closet. As she grew older, Vera tired of the ranch's seclusion. She offered to sell it to the U.S. government for use as a park. The million-dollar-plus price tag was too steep, but it was chump change to billionaire Howard Hughes, who bought the ranch from Vera three months before she died.

After Vera's death in 1967, the ring went up for auction. Bidding over $300,000 dollars, actor Richard Burton was the highest bidder. He gave the Krupp diamond to his wife Elizabeth Taylor, who wore it proudly, even claiming at one point that it was her favorite piece.

Of the ring, Elizabeth Taylor once said, "My ring gives me the strangest feeling for beauty. "With its sparks of red and white and blue and purple, and on and on, really, it sort of hums with its own beatific life."

After Elizabeth Taylor's death in 2011, the Krupp Diamond was renamed the Taylor-Burton Diamond. It was purchased by a South Korean businessman, who was bidding on behalf of E-land World, a South Korean company. The bidding stopped at $8.8 million. E-Land World planned to exhibit the diamond ring at E-World, an amusement park in Daegu.

Home Invasion at Mr. Las Vegas's Place

Known as the "Midnight Idol," "Mr. Las Vegas," and "Mr. Entertainment," Wayne Newton is well known and well respected in Las Vegas. The singer has been a part of the Las Vegas entertainment scene for over sixty years. At twenty-one, he recorded the hit song "*Danke Schön*" in 1962. Three years later, he had another hit with "Red Roses for a Blue Lady." He has appeared in several movies and TV shows, including *Bonanza* and *I Love Lucy*. He is a star, and stars generally have their homes well-protected and guarded against those who would steal from them or do them harm.

Newton himself has a CCW (a concealed weapon permit), and like others of his stature, he has the latest and best gadgetry and alarms protecting his home. Newton does not seem like someone who would be the victim of a home robbery, and yet he was—not once but twice. The Newton family home was burglarized by the same people—twice within ten days.

The first burglary took place while Newton and his family were away in New York. Ten days later, Newton; his wife, Kathleen McCrone Newton; and their seventeen-year-old daughter were returning from an evening out when they came home to find Wesley Hosea Martin and an unidentified man helping themselves to the singer's personal property. Newton's daughter walked in on them. The panic-stricken teenager raced to her father, "Daddy someone is in your dressing room," she said.

The accomplice turned to run when he realized the mansions residents had arrived. Martin raised a tire iron at Mrs. Newton as if to hit her, and was set upon by the family's two large dogs. He struck one of the animals injuring it and knocking its teeth out, and then joined his pal in fleeing the scene.

Martin was caught a week later when he tried to pawn some of the singer's belongings. A neighbor's door camera provided further evidence that the police had the right man. His accomplice had still not been arrested when Wesley Hosea Martin went to trial.

On June 18, 2019, almost a year to the day of the robbery, Wayne Newton, his wife, and his daughter went to court to see that justice was done. Newton strode into the courtroom using a cane, set to testify about the harrowing experience he and his family had endured the previous year,

Wayne Newton's wife and daughter also testified about the night their palatial home was invaded. Luckily the entertainer and his family were not seriously injured or harmed during the crime.

Since that night, Newton has improved and upgraded his security systems. He has also hired armed guards so that he and his family will never go through another harrowing night like they did in June 2018.

Wesley Hosea Martin was found guilty of twelve felonies. He will be incarcerated at the Nevada state prison for a long while.

Unfilial—Brookey Lee West

> *How sharper than a serpent's tooth it is to have a thankless child.*
>
> *William Shakespeare*

Early on, Christine Smith seemed destined to live a hard life on the seedy side of town. Still, no one could have guessed that she would end up stuffed in a garbage can in a Las Vegas storage unit, but she did. What is worse, she was placed there by her very own daughter, Brookey Lee West.

Like that of her mother, Brookey Lee West's childhood was anything but idyllic. Christine Smith had never been the loving parent she might have been. She was young and attractive. She was also too busy falling in and out of love to spend much time facing the responsibilities of motherhood and taking care of her two children—Brookey and her brother, Travis. By the time they were grown, it was too late for her maternal instincts to kick in.

To say that life was unkind to Christine Smith is an understatement. By the time she died at sixty-eight, she was a helpless old woman suffering the effects of a hard life spent drinking and smoking heavily. She also suffered from Alzheimer's. She was living in an apartment in Las Vegas and she was happy. She had made peace with the past. Life was good. She had friends and her daughter came from San Jose to see her regularly. That is more than she could say for her son Travis. She had not heard from him in a very long time—no one had.

As a young woman, Christine was wild. Her focus was on her love life and not her children. Jealous of her married lover, she confronted him in a Bakersfield bar, shooting to kill. She missed. The crime still meant a fourteen-year stretch in the California women's institute. She had given no thought to her children or who might take care of them.

With their mother in prison, Brookey and her brother were left to fend for themselves. And fend they did, until Christine was released, after serving only two years. Like she always had, she picked up where she left off and continued dragging her children along from one place to another. No child deserves such a mother. Yet, no mother deserves a child that would stuff her into a 45-gallon drum and leave her to die. Clearly, both Christine and Brookey were losers in the mother–daughter sweepstakes.

On February 5, 2001, there was that horrid stench. The manager of the mini-storage caught another whiff as he again walked past unit 317. Curious, he opened the cluttered unit and saw the large garbage drum with dark-colored liquid oozing from it; he had found the source of the smell. Certain that whatever it was, it was not good, the man called the police. One of the crime scene analysts knew exactly what the odor meant. "The unmistakable smell of death," he called it.

A blood test confirmed that the contents of the drum were human. Obviously, the death was not a suicide. The manager checked his records and gave police the names of the two women who had rented the unit three years earlier: Christine Smith and Brookey West. Foraging through the items in the storage unit, police found a wallet and other items belonging to one of them.

The investigation turned up neighbors of Christine Smith, who told the story of Christine and her daughter who worked in San Jose. One night without so much as a farewell, Christine packed up and went to stay with her son in California; at least that was the story Brookey told. However, the curious wondered why some of Christine's things were in the resident's dumpster.

It was beginning to look like Brookey Lee West had killed her own mother. The mess in the garbage can was identified as having once been Christine Smith. Travis Smith had not been seen or heard from in years; how had Brookey taken their mother to him? Then too, it was none other than Brookey Lee West's fingerprints on the tape that had held the lid on the garbage can tight.

Four days after the discovery at the storage unit, Brookey Lee West was arrested for the murder of Christine Smith. It is not every day that anyone is accused of killing their own mother. Our society is fascinated with outlying monsters, and the media glommed onto the sensational story. Brookey insisted her mother had died of natural causes and not knowing what else to do she had stuff the body into the garbage can. Yet why had a plastic bag been wrapped around the dead woman's head? Also, why was Brookey Lee West still availing herself of mother's social security checks? Brookey Lee West remained a suspect in the June 1994 death of her ex-husband, Howard Simon St. John.

West's trial began on July 3, 2001. Explanation might have worked, if only science was not able to look at maggots and blowflies that have a penchant for rotting flesh. In testimony, a forensic entomologist contrasted the different type maggot or blowfly that would have been present if Christine Smith had been alive or dead when placed in the container. In spite of what Brookey Lee West insisted, he believed that Smith had been alive at the time.

On July 19, 2001, after two hours of deliberation, the jury found Brookey Lee West guilty of first-degree murder. In sentencing her to life without the possibility of parole, District Court Judge Donald Mosely said, "While I think everyone would agree putting someone's mother in a garbage can to bury her is bizarre, placing her in there conscious to suffocate her is not only bizarre, it's criminal. You are sentenced to life without the possibility of parole. That's all."

In 2003, she appealed her conviction to the Nevada Supreme Court. She lost the appeal. In 2012, she made an unsuccessful attempt to escape the Florence McClure Women's Correctional Center in Las Vegas. She resides there today.

Willis Obenauer's Kneecaps

Las Vegas is a major city and one of the fastest-growing cities in the country, but it is a small town in some ways. One of those is gossip. It is hard to keep a secret in a small town; it is even harder to keep a secret in a casino (large or small). This comes as no surprise to anyone who has ever punched a time clock in a casino. Backyard gossip has nothing on casino gossip. The juicier and better gossip flies on its own wings, transforming as it goes from one end of the place to the other, regardless of size.

Hotel manager Willis Obenauer played a part in some of the juiciest gossip to ever hit the help's hall of the Hacienda. Obenauer was on the good side of fifty and athletic. Like any other supervisor, there were those who liked the acerbic Willis Obenauer and there were those who disliked him immensely. One of those was bell captain Frank LaPena. Obenauer was a stickler for the rules, which, according to casino gossip, LaPena flouted in the pursuit of extra cash.

The favored method was said to be a system in which unoccupied rooms were made available for prostitutes and their customers in exchange for a cut of their earnings. When Obenauer stopped LaPena's side hustle, he gained the bell captain's wrath.

Two days after Thanksgiving 1973, shortly after midnight, Gerald Weakland and an accomplice waited for Obenauer to get into his car and drive to his apartment. They followed him home. Once at the apartment, the men forced Obenauer back into his car and drove out into the desert. There, Weakland pulled Obenauer from the car and beat him with a 9-mm pistol until he was nearly senseless. The *coup de grâce* was delivered by a bullet from .38-caliber pistol to each of his kneecaps. They left him injured there in the desert and drove away in his car.

Four months later, Gerald Weakland was arrested for the murder of Hilda Krause and he started talking. He was guilty of kidnapping and assault on Obenauer, but only because Frank LaPena had given him $500 to do the job. LaPena's dislike of Obenauer was immense. Obenauer needed a lesson. Weakland and his accomplice were also employed the Hacienda. They claimed that on the night of the attack, LaPena had pointed out Obenauer to them and given them a pair of weighted gloves, the better to beat Willis Obenauer.

On the word of Weakland and his accomplice Robert Webb, Frank LaPena was arrested and charged with second-degree kidnapping and battery with the use of a deadly weapon. Obenauer testified that a week or two before the incident, he saw Frank LaPena talking with Gerald Weakland. He also testified that he and Frank LaPena did not get along and he had had to cite LaPena for infraction of hotel rules. A bellman offered testimony in which he stated that LaPena had told him that he would like to tear Obenauer's heart out.

Gerald Weakland's ex-wife also testified to seeing LaPena and Weakland together shortly before the attack on Obenauer. It was at a Tower of Pizza restaurant, she explained, and Weakland told her to leave them alone while they talked. She stated that after the assault, Weakland told her to return the lead-filled gloves to LaPena. She returned them to Frank LaPena at the Hacienda Hotel.

At the trial, the accomplice's girlfriend testified that he had told her Obenauer was attacked at the behest of Weakland's brother. Other witnesses testified that LaPena was actually at home and not at the Hacienda, pointing out Obenauer as Weakland claimed.

At LaPena's trial, Weakland refused to testify. This would seem to be his *modus operandi*—confess, point the finger at someone else, and then refuse to testify. Eventually, he did testify that LaPena paid him to beat up Obenauer.

The jury found Frank LaPena guilty of second-degree kidnapping and battery with a deadly weapon in connection with the abduction of Obenauer. The Nevada Supreme Court later overturned the conviction because evidence did not back up Weakland's claim that LaPena was involved. Weakland's next crime, the coldblooded murder of Hilda Krause, was committed a month after kidnapping and shooting Willis Obenauer.

Everything but the Money

From the time she was a young woman, Hilda Krause had worked hard. Life had not always been easy for Hilda; she had scrimped and saved, divorced and remarried. After years of running a Bowling Green Kentucky restaurant, she and her second husband, Marvin, went to Cuba where she bought and operated a Havana casino, which was a financial success. She was meeting famous people and making a lot of money. Then, in 1959, Fidel Castro and his communist regime overthrew military dictator Fulgencio Batista and took control of the tiny nation, forcing the Krauses out of Cuba forever. The astute businesswoman had her wits and most of her money. The Krauses relocated to Las Vegas and invested in Caesars Palace.

Hilda and Marvin had been married for thirty years, but the one thing that brought purpose and meaning to Hilda Krause's life was her only child, a son (from a previous marriage) who would twenty years hence be elected a justice on the Kentucky State Supreme Court. Her life had been good and financially rewarding. Even as Hilda slept peacefully in the king-size bed she and Marvin shared, her life was coming to a cruel and violent close.

Marvin was an early riser. This day would be no different. Hilda did not wake when he got up and ready for work. She seldom did. She was still sleeping when he walked out into the garage where their brand new his-and-hers Eldorados were parked. The Krauses lived comfortably, in a townhome at 2995 Pinehurst Street, situated behind the walls of the Las Vegas Country Club Estates, a gated community in which wealthy entertainers and politicians lived—a safe place.

On Monday, January 14, 1974, it was the dead of winter, which meant the day would typically get no warmer than 58 degrees—cold by Vegas standards. It was around 5 a.m. The sun would not rise for a few more hours and darkness still enveloped the city. Those who worked swing shift were just heading to bed, and Marvin Krause was ready to greet the day as day shift slot manager at Caesars Palace. He lifted the garage door and stepped back to his gleaming Caddy with its personalized plates, "MARV." At that time, not every other car on the road had personalized plates; only those who could afford the little bit of look-at-me luxury bothered with them. Marvin was proud of those plates. They represented that he was somebody special. He liked that. Also, it did not bother him a wit that the money he enjoyed had come to him by way of his wife, Hilda. Still, it is always good to let the world know that you are special. As he opened the car door, two men, their faces covered by masks, rushed at him.

One of the men grabbed Marvin, roughly holding on to him while the other man quickly closed the garage door. Marvin Krause would not be going to work today after all. Life had just gone sideways for Mr. and Mrs. Krause. The men pushed him back into his house toward the bedroom where Hilda Krause still slept, unaware of the savagery that had entered the sanctuary of her home.

"Wake up!" One of the men ordered the sleeping Hilda jostling her, roughly. Barely awake, the elderly woman struggled to sit up as she tried to make sense of what was happening to her. "Get dressed!" He snapped at her, watching as she slowly pulled a blouse on over her nightgown. Thus dressed and fully awake, Hilda Krause was gagged with a scarf, tied up with an electric cord, and left alone in her room. Marvin was dragged to the next room and tied up as well.

With the Krauses securely out of the way, the men pawed through the couple's belongings, taking whatever jewelry and cash they could find. One of the intruders pawed through a kitchen drawer until he found a suitable knife. Then, with knife in hand, he calmly walked back upstairs to the room where Hilda was tied up. Without a word, he strangled the helpless woman, slashed her throat, and then stabbed her in the back. He left the knife in the dead woman's back and stepped into the next bedroom where Marvin Krause was tied up. He struck the old man twice, knocking him unconscious. The job was done. He raced to the garage where his accomplice waited. One of them lifted the garage door while the other started Marvin's Caddy. It would serve as their getaway car. The Caddy would not be so shiny and new when it was returned to Marvin.

After the assailants were gone, Marvin Krause struggled free of the electrical cord and stumbled into the next room to find his wife dead, still tied with electrical cord. In murder cases, the spouse is always the first person crime investigators focus their suspicion upon. This does not speak well of love and marriage; nonetheless, it is a fact. Still, Marvin had been battered by the killer. When asked, he could think of no reason why his life had been spared. Neither could investigators. Why would the men leave a witness behind who could identify them? No one likes to think about innocent people being robbed and killed in their own homes, especially in an upscale place like Las Vegas Country Club Estates, in the dead of winter when the heat was on.

Even in a town that thrives on gambling, it is stunning how often luck plays a hand in solving a murder, and luck seemed to be on the side of investigators when a confidential informant came forward with a name. An acquaintance by the name of Gerald Weakland had asked him to go with him on a robbery at the Country Club Estates. Weakland, who had been a local high school football star, was arrested the next day. He too, had a story to tell, strange as it was. Although he was confessing to slitting the elderly Hilda Krause's throat, he said he had been paid to do so. After assurances that he would be given a deal, he said that an acquaintance named Frank LaPena and his girlfriend, Rosalie Maxwell, had paid him $1,000 up front and promised another $10,000 when the deed was done.

Here is where the story gets so convoluted it almost defies logic. LaPena was a bell captain at the Hacienda and Rosalie was a cocktail waitress supervisor at Caesars Palace. Apparently, Rosalie agreed with poet William Cowper's line from his 1785 poem "The Task," "variety's the very spice of life" as Frank was not the only man in her life. Rosalie was a married woman who was also dating Marvin Krause, slot manager at Caesars. Marvin was sixty-four, his wife Hilda was seventy-one, and Rosalie was, at forty-five, the younger woman.

Weakland told investigators that LaPena and Maxwell had reasoned that if they could get Hilda out of the way, Marvin would marry Rosalie and she would then be able to bankroll whatever dreams her lover LaPena might have. On Weakland's word, LaPena and Maxwell were arrested for the murder of Hilda Krause. During interrogation, they readily admitted to being lovers. Rosalie Maxwell would say of Krause that he was her live one while Frank LaPena was the love of her life. Marvin Krause may have seen the relationship with Rosalie as mutual and romantic, but she did not. He was just someone who had money (albeit his wife's) and was willing to throw some her way.

Weakland, the confessed killer, got himself a sweet deal. He would be out of prison in seven years. After the longest preliminary hearing in Nevada's history, Rosalie Maxwell got herself acquitted. By all accounts, she was a gorgeous woman. This and the fact that Weakland refused to testify against her at trial probably swayed the jury. Frank LaPena was not so lucky. He would spend more time in prison than Weakland, the actual killer. During his twenty-five years in the Nevada state prison, LaPena never gave up trying to clear his name and gain his freedom. His case went to the Nevada Supreme Court five times in those twenty-five years. While he did so, Gerald Weakland was paroled again and again—at least six times. He just could not seem to obey the rules. He did not pay his supervision fees and he had a minor scrape with the law.

In 2003, Frank LaPena went before the Nevada state pardons board, asking for release from prison. One of those who spoke on LaPena's behalf was former Nevada State Supreme Court Justice Al Gunderson, who said that he was more convinced than ever that LaPena should never have been charged.

Marvin Krause died of a stroke in 1975, a year after his wife's murder. Rosalie Maxwell died of cancer on February 25, 1997.

In April 2016, an obituary appeared in the *Reno Gazette Journal* for sixty-eight-year-old Gerald Weakland, who passed away at his home on April 2. He graduated from Las Vegas High in 1965, then won a state boxing championship and turned professional. He did cabinetry and woodworking, loved his family, and volunteered at the Salvation

Army. There was no a mention of Willis Obenauer's kneecaps or the elderly Hilda Krause and of the morning he cruelly slashed her throat, but then, that is not something relatives share about their deceased loved ones.

Frank LaPena

Today, Frank LaPena is eighty-one years old. He works at the Mob Museum, where he entertains patrons with stories of the mob while referring to himself as a mob specialist. He does not explain exactly what it is a mob specialist did. Frank was a 2018 recipient of LVCVA Hospitality Hero Award. He is friendly and charismatic and looks a good twenty years younger than his actual age. He and his wife, Betty, share their home with a rescue dog that goes by the name of Samson and an elderly tuxedo cat that does not particularly care for strangers. She is one of those felines you pet at your own risk.

In June 2019, I met with Frank LaPena and asked him about the Obenauer and Krause cases. I showed him a draft of that part of this book that pertains to him. He slipped on his glasses and quickly read it. "This isn't true," he said. "I didn't run girls at the Hacienda." He then gave me the name of the person who had. "When I found out what he was doing, I told him I'd fire him if he didn't stop."

On November 6, 2019, Frank LaPena received a conditional pardon from the Nevada Board of Pardons. When Nevada Governor Steve Sisolak (chairman of the board) asked LaPena why he had not sought a full pardon that would have restored his right to own a gun, LaPena said that guns only get you in trouble. All he wanted to do was to be able to travel without seeking permission. "I'm going to Disneyland." LaPena quipped after being granted his pardon. Frank LaPena is in the process of writing a book about his life and this case called *The Goddess and the Bell Captain*.

Suitcase

The idea of disposing of bodies in suitcases is not new. Winnie Ruth Judd probably was not the first to have done so, but she is the first to have gained worldwide recognition for her murderous misdeed. Winnie Ruth traveled by rail from Arizona to Los Angeles in 1931 with her victims' bodies stuffed into trunks—certainly not a well-thought-out idea, she got stopped by the stench and the gore that oozed forth. Nearly ninety years later, killers still dispose of bodies in such a fashion.

On August 12, 2013, no matter how much Carl Simon denied doing so, the trio believed he had stolen drug money, and after battering him with a liquor bottle, stabbing him with scissors, and whipping him with a belt, Emilio Arenas and Peyton Hemingway could not believe their victim was still alive. To remedy the situation, they stripped him naked, and while a female friend looked on, Arenas stuffed fifty-year-old Simon in his own suitcase and plunged it into a bathtub at Budget Suites on Boulder Highway. While Simon drowned, Emilio Arenas cruelly sang along with Ozzy Osbourne's 1980 hit "Crazy Train" on the cell phone. Simon's body was found in a dumpster 6 miles from where he was murdered.

The murder was dubbed the "Crazy Train Murder." Three people were arrested and charged with murder; the woman who witnessed the slaying turned against her friends, telling it all in an effort to get a reduced sentence. She was charged with second-degree murder, as was Hemingway. However, the prosecution wanted a death penalty for Arenas, who had a long criminal record; he was sentenced to life without the possibility of parole.

Ulysis Cesar Molina died on Christmas Day 2016. Filled with yuletide joy, Molina went to the apartment of a woman he was dating. Molina did not know that she was also romantically involved with Anthony Newton. When Newton showed up at the apartment, all yuletide joy vanished. He accused Molina of sleeping with his wife and slammed him to the floor. Newton was beating Molina badly when George Macaperdas came knocking at the door. Now it was two against one and Macaperdas was angry as well. He had heard that Molina had been sleeping with Macaperdas's sister, who happened to be Anthony Newton's wife.

Newton and Macaperdas tied Molina up with a cord. Then Newton stood on the helpless Molina's throat until he was dead. They stripped Molina's body and wrapped it in a sheet. The two men then drove to another location where they would dismember the body and stuff parts of it in a suitcase. They then drove to a vacant lot where they poured gasoline on the suitcase and set it on fire.

Two days later, a homeless woman was awakened by the sounds of a car's doors banging. She listened as something was dragged across the vacant lot that she was camped in. She waited until the next day to see what had been dumped nearby. Carefully opening the charred duffle bag, she discovered a man's hacked legs and torso. It would take DNA tests to identify the body as that of Ulysis Cesar Molina. That was when a witness came forward to tell the sordid tale of Molina's murder.

idnight on October 22, 1979 forty-six-year-old Jesse Walter
_p dressed in a white shirt and prison denims and calmly walked into
Nevada's gas chamber, ready to accept his fate. He had been convicted of
murdering David Ballard, who had foolhardily got involved in Bishop's
robbery of the El Morocco Casino five days before Christmas 1977.

Bishop needed drug money. He strode to the cashier's cage and, showing
his gun, he told the terrified cashier, "I'm here to rob the place." The woman
looked at the gun and screamed. Ballard, who was enjoying his newlywed
status, rushed up to see if he could help. A pit boss pulled his gun and shot
at Bishop, who returned fire. Realizing he was in danger, Ballard tried to
run. Bishop shot him in the back. In describing the incident, a witness said
that Bishop shot the twenty-two-year-old man, "like a dog."

David Ballard had come from Baltimore to be married in Las Vegas.
He had only been a husband for three hours when Bishop shot him and
the El Morocco Casino Hotel pit boss. The pit boss lived. Ballard died
a few days later. It was all for $278, but heroin addict Bishop was not
finished. He committed several other robberies and crimes throughout
Las Vegas before he was finally caught in Boulder City. The Korean
War veteran confessed to Ballard's murder and was convicted of
first-degree murder.

While his attorneys and civil rights groups tried to fight his death
sentence, Bishop was resigned. He refused appeals and would not fight for
his life. On the day of his execution, Bishop ordered steak for his last meal
and ate with gusto. To the very end, he refused to ask for an appeal. While
being strapped into the execution chair in the gas chamber, Bishop's final
words to Prison Warden Charles Wolff were, "This is one more step down
the road of life that I've been heading for all my life."

When he heard the pellets drop, Jesse Walter Bishop smiled and inhaled
deeply. Nine minutes later, he was dead. After witnessing the execution,
Warden Wolff said of Bishop, "He was like an iceman, tough as nails
to the end." After the execution, Nevada District Judge Paul Goldman,
one of the three judges who sentenced Bishop to death, came forward
to tell of visiting with Bishop in prison two months earlier. During their
conversation, Bishop told Goldman that he had been involved in eighteen
contract killings that involved drugs.

Jesse Bishop's execution set two Nevada records—he was the first
person to be executed since capital punishment was reinstated by the
Nevada legislature in 1977, and he was also the last person to be executed
in Nevada's gas chamber. In 1979, Nevada would adopt lethal injection as
its method of execution.

Carroll Cole—The First

Carroll Cole was executed by lethal injection on December 6, 1985. Earlier, the serial killer had agreed that his brain could be studied by science; so, shortly after Cole was declared dead, his brain was removed by Las Vegas neurosurgeon Lonnie Hammargren, who found no lesions or other abnormalities—score one for the nurture side of the nurture *v.* nature debate. Like several other serial killers, Carroll Cole had suffered traumatic childhood abuse. Yet his brain was normal; there was no physical reason for his lifelong wanton killing spree.

Cole killed his first victim at the age of ten when he drowned a ten-year-old playmate for making fun of Cole's name, saying "Carroll" was a girl's name. Enraged, the murderous youngster held the other boy underwater until he was sure he was dead. Years later, Cole would confess to the killing everyone believed was an accident.

Carroll Cole began killing as an adult driven to murder by his hatred of an abusive mother. His *modus operandi* was the same; he would pick up women in bars, have sex with them, then strangle them to death. From California to Texas, it is believed that Cole killed at least fifteen women. Although he admitted to murdering a Las Vegas prostitute in 1977, it was the murder of Marie Cushman at the Casbah Hotel in Las Vegas in 1979 that earned him the death penalty. At the time of the 1977 murder, Nevada had not yet reinstated its death penalty. Carroll Cole was the first person to be executed by lethal injection in the state of Nevada.

Sebastian Bridges—Going Out in Style

Most condemned people walk into the death chamber wearing standard prison attire—a white t-shirt and jeans—but not Sebastian Bridges; he asked for, and received, permission to dress more formally for the occasion. On April 22, 2001, Sebastian was escorted to his execution wearing a dashing double-breasted Pierre Cardin suit and tie with shiny black shoes. The South African nationalist had been convicted of murdering his ex-wife's boyfriend, twenty-seven-year-old Hunter Blanchard, in the desert outside of Las Vegas in 1997.

Bridges met Laurie, a nurse, while serving time in a California prison. They fell in love, and upon his release in 1993, they were married. The marriage lasted four years. Fleeing Bridges's physical abuse, Laurie moved to Las Vegas. There, she divorced Bridges and met Hunter Blanchard, also a nurse.

When Bridges found her, he was furious but pretended to be okay with her new romance. He tried to trade his truck to Blanchard if he would end his relationship with Laurie. When that did not work, he agreed to drive Laurie and Blanchard to the place where he had stored Laurie's belongings, with no hard feelings. The unsuspecting lovers got in his vehicle and Bridges drove far out into the desert. He stopped the car and displayed his gun. "You're gonna kill me now, aren't you?" Hunter Blanchard asked, as they got out of the car. "I trusted you! I trusted you!" Blanchard said. Without a word, Sebastian Bridges shot the other man in the stomach.

Laurie raced to the wounded man. "I'm so sorry. I love you! I love you with all my heart." She cried trying to comfort the dying man. Bridges wrapped Blanchard's body in plastic and tossed it in the trunk. Forcing Laurie back in the car, he drove toward California. There he took a new shovel from the truck, dug a shallow grave, and tossed the lifeless body of Hunter Blanchard in.

"I killed nobody! I killed nobody!" Sebastian Bridges yelled in his last living moments. Hunter Blanchard's father, who had come all the way from Tennessee to witness the execution of his son's killer, eyed Bridges dispassionately; he was a cold-blooded killer without remorse.

An Innocent Man and the Murder of a Trapeze Artist

> *He'd fly through the air with the greatest of ease,*
> *That daring young man on the flying trapeze*

Fred Steese was an innocent man who spent twenty-one years in a Nevada prison for a murder he did not commit. On June 4, 1992, Gerard (Jerry) Soules was brutally murdered, stabbed more than thirty times, in his trailer home at the Silver Nugget Camperland RV Park. Soules's nude body was found in the blood-spattered bathroom, his throat slashed, and his face covered by a towel. The trailer had been tossed, his TV and VCR had been stolen, and his mattress was blood-soaked. The killer had not harmed any of Soules's dogs.

Soules's career quite literally went to the dogs. At sixteen, the adventuresome Soules left his home in Michigan and joined the circus, dreaming of becoming an aerialist. He was agile and strong. Through hard work and practice, his ability and confidence grew. While in his early twenties, he worked as an aerialist for Barnum and Bailey's, Ringling Brothers, and other circuses. Soules was talented and he knew how to entertain the crowd. He quickly became a star.

Billed as the "star of stars on the high trapeze," the flamboyant Soules commanded the center ring and wore heavily jewel-encrusted aerialist capes that he had designed and sewn himself. YouTube and other sources offer clips of Soules back in the day, his heels grasping the bar as he swings 50 feet above the crowd. When a near-fatal accident ended his aerialist career, the fearless trapeze artist had already performed before thousands of people around the world, including the queen of England. Yet the accident had taken his confidence, and without that, his days of dazzling the crowds were over.

However, Gerard Soules was not a quitter. Even though he could no longer work as an aerialist, his love for the circus and performing would never end. He would entertain audiences with a different act. There had always been performing animals in the circus. Aside from the elephants, horses, and tigers, there were poodles. Soules decided that he would train poodles to perform. Using his sewing skills, he designed and made elaborate and bedazzling costumes for his poodles. This began his "Poodles de Paree," cute little poodles adorned in sequins as they twirled and pranced around the ring. The canine troupe quickly became a hit with circus audiences everywhere. Soules was back in the spotlight when he and his poodles were booked on several television shows, also becoming regulars at the Ice Capades.

Las Vegas offers opportunity for anyone in the entertainment industry. Ever since its opening in 1968, Circus Circus added something new to the mix by offering jobs for circus performers. In 1992, Soules made his way to Las Vegas with his Poodles de Paree. It did not take him very long to land a job at Circus Circus. Audiences adored Soules and his prancing poodles in their spangled costumes, so Soules was content. He and his poodles had a home in his 45-foot trailer that he parked in Circus Circus RV Park. Then, he was informed that he would have to move his trailer elsewhere.

Shortly after moving to a different location, Soules met Fred Steese. The pair became lovers shortly after Soules took the homeless and much younger Steese under his wing and into his life. Soules was lonely. His longtime partner had died, leaving him hungry for companionship and love. He had recently fired his assistant Alexander Kolupaev, who helped with the dogs but wanted no part of a romance. Steese was alone as well. Soon, Steese was Soules's assistant in his dog act at Circus Circus's casino. Just when it seemed like life was finally turning around for both of them, Steese was told that he needed a work permit to work for the casino.

This is standard as no one is permitted to work in a casino without a work card that establishes them legally. Steese realized that he would not be able to obtain one as he had violated parole in Florida. He told Soules,

"Listen, I'm going to go ahead and move on because there ain't no sense in me being here, because I can't make no money."

With those words, he wished his benefactor well and left the state of Nevada. Six days later, Soules failed to show up for work. Phone calls to him went unanswered. This was unlike Jerry; he was reliable and never missed work. His boss was concerned. He drove to the RV Park, grabbed a security guard, and walked into a blood-soaked horror.

As he had been the most recent lover, and the man who moved out days before the murder, suspicion fell on Steese. Drug-addled and exhausted, Steese cracked during interrogation and confessed to killing Soules. Convicted of the murder of Gerard Soules, Steese continued to proclaim his innocence. He had not even been in Nevada when Soules was killed and, his attorneys argued, the prosecutors were aware of it. Still they claimed that it was not Steese that witnesses placed in Idaho but his look-a-like brother, Robert. A witness who saw a man around Soule's trailer described him as a redhead with receding hairline. Incidentally, this description fit Alexander Kolupaev, who was not questioned and had since been deported. In 2005, thirteen years after his death, Soules was inducted into the International Circus Hall of Fame as aerialist and dog trainer.

On November 8, 2017, the Nevada Board of Pardons issued a full pardon for Fred Steese.

"Shut Up and Don't Call Me a Bitch"

On May 4, 2018, in North Las Vegas, nineteen-year-old Dymund Ellis was very serious about watching her television show. Her roommate, twenty-five-year-old, Jason Trevon Ernst was not. He kept talking. Even when she asked him to shut up, Ernst continued to talk. Finally, Ellis yelled, "Shut up!"

"Shut up yourself, bitch!" Ernst answered.

Ellis jumped up and ran into the kitchen for a knife. "Go ahead, call me a bitch again." She threatened.

"Bitch." He smirked. She plunged the knife into his chest, hitting his heart and killing him instantly. Jason Trevon Ernst would no longer be calling her, or anyone else, a bitch.

The HOV Lane

The HOV (high-occupancy vehicle) freeway lane is less congested and thus quicker. It is clearly designated that there must be at least two people in the vehicle in order to use the lane; those solo drivers who think they can zip on through without being stopped are wrong. Solo drivers caught using the lane in Las Vegas will be stopped and ticketed with no questions asked.

One summer afternoon, a clever hearse driver reasoned that he should be able to use the HOV lane. After all, he was transporting a deceased person, albeit in a funeral home minivan. The Nevada highway trooper disagreed; he did have another person in the vehicle, but a person can only be counted as a plus-one if they are alive and breathing—the dead are considered cargo.

In this case, Lady Luck was also riding with the hearse driver, though she did not count as a passenger either. Instead of being ticketed, the driver was given a warning and told to pull out of the HOV.

Just Another Naked Guy

With an average temperature of 80 degrees, there is no denying that Las Vegas, on the edge of the Mojave Desert, is a hot place where topless dancers are on full display every day and every night in various locations in the city; however, public nudity on the streets of Sin City is another thing entirely. Maybe the heat is the reason, though maybe not.

The phenomenon of a naked man at odds with police officers is not a Las Vegas-only occurrence. It happens all across the country. On April 2, 2018, a naked man broke into a Las Vegas home for no apparent reason. The owner fled the house and called police. When they arrived, the man climbed out onto the roof and refused to come down. After successful SWAT negotiations, the man was taken into custody.

On January 24, 2017, a fifty-year-old transient, who walked naked into the pool area of the Gold Strike Casino in Jean (31 miles south of Las Vegas), was not so lucky. The man had stabbed himself numerous times and was not deterred by the bean bags police fired at him. He raised his knife and charged one of the officers who fired at him, killing him instantly.

In August 2019, police were called on a naked man who was throwing rocks outside his home in the Summerlin area. He ran inside the house and started tossing things from a second-story window, as police arrived. After an hour-long standoff, he was dressed and escorted to jail.

Bad Times at Baby's

The Nevada Gaming Control Board is in control. Any licensee or gaming establishment that forgets this will regret the lapse of memory as they will pay a hefty fine at best or risk losing a license at worst. This lesson was driven home at the Hard Rock Hotel Casino in 2002, when the hotel casino's hip nightclub Baby's ran afoul of the gaming control board.

Baby's nightclub opened in 1998. Located in the basement of the Hard Rock, the purple-and-blue-themed nightclub was where a fun-loving young crowd gathered to listen to a variety of music genres, to drink, and to party. Apparently, a whole lot more was going on than simply drinking and conviviality. State Gaming Control Board investigators had had their eyes on Baby's for months following complaints of bawdy behavior. What they found would ultimately cost the Hard Rock $100,000 in fines.

Three separate times, gaming control investigators witnessed, and later caught on surveillance cameras, patrons engaged in what they deemed inappropriate sexual conduct in a private seating section that was in full view of the public. These sexual incidents were also in view of employees, including security guards. Unlike lap dances (which were illegal in Clark County at that time), the overt sexual activity is a violation of gaming regulations.

The president of Hard Rock agreed to make corrective actions and a settlement was reached. The $100,000 was paid and the Hard Rock promised to sin no more. Baby's nightclub was closed in 2004. However, this was not the end of troubles for the Hard Rock Hotel Casino.

Death on the Blue Diamond

Nevada State Route 160, known locally as the Blue Diamond Road, runs from Las Vegas toward Pahrump. The amount of fatalities that have occurred on Blue Diamond makes it one of the area's deadliest roads.

On Wednesday, January 26, 2006, it was not quite noon when retired porn actress Anna Malle (Anna Hotop-Stout) climbed into the passenger seat of her friend's Dodge Stratus. Hotop-Stout was thirty-eight years old and trying to live a normal life. In her career as porn star Anna Malle, she had appeared in over 200 films; she had a slew of fans and was well-liked in the industry. Yet age is more than a number in the entertainment industry. She was working at a local Las Vegas department store, making far less than she had in porn but happy.

In 1955, James Dean did a public service announcement about the dangers of speeding mere weeks before he met his death while speeding on a California highway. Thirteen years later, on January 1, 1968, seatbelts became mandatory in the U.S. as they save lives. Not wearing a seatbelt is a minor offense that earns you a ticket and a fine in Nevada. However, Hotop-Stout, for whatever reason, did not buckle her seatbelt on this day.

The Stratus was traveling west. Just beyond Rainbow Blvd., the driver eased up on the gas and entered the eastbound lane in an attempt to make a U-turn. A pickup truck came barreling down the road from the opposite direction, tragically too late to stop. The truck plowed into the car, killing the beautiful Anna Malle. Seven years after her death, Anna Malle was inducted into the Adult Video News Hall of Fame in 2013.

Hard Times at the Hard Rock

Sex, drugs, and rock 'n' roll do not mix in a gaming establishment. In 2011, just nine years after paying a $100,000 fine to the Nevada Gaming Control Board, the Hard Rock Hotel Casino was in hot water again, and the fine was steeper.

Gaming Control Board investigators and Metro officers were conducting an undercover operation at the Hard Rock Hotel Casino. During this time, they discovered marijuana and cocaine being sold by employees, who offered the use of private restrooms for drug use and sex. Although the Hard Rock was diligent in trying to prevent illegal activity on the premises, it is hard to find good help, harder still to keep an eye on every one of them at all times, and the Hard Rock definitely had a few bad ones.

In an after-the-fact random drug test, thirteen employees failed. Some of these people were in the security department. This did not help the Hard Rock with its immediate problem with the Gaming Control Board that had filed an eight-count complaint against the establishment. The settlement fine for these counts was $650,000 and a reminder of how close the establishment was to a license revocation hearing.

Out with the old, in with the new, Las Vegas style—on November 3, 2019, the Hard Rock Hotel Casino closed its doors. Its trademark 82-foot-tall guitar was set to be demolished and plans were underway for remodeling, with a new casino hotel to take its place.

Once Upon a Time at Pussycat a Go-Go

During the 1960s, the Pussycat a Go-Go was the place on the Strip that the young mod set went to see and be seen. Up-and-coming groups appeared here while and up-and-coming entertainers partied. With dancing, live music, and go-go dancers (long-haired young women in tall white boots and miniskirts), the young crowd did not want to go anyplace else in Las Vegas.

The Vietnam War, a society that was rapidly changing, thanks to its younger generation of flower children, made the late 1960s a time of unrest. Among those who took a dim view of the state of the world was songwriter, vocalist, and member of the Doors, Jim Morrison. Morrison and the Doors were thrust to stardom in the music world with their 1967 song "Light My Fire," which was followed by "Hello, I Love You" in 1968. Both songs became number one hits in the U.S. and Canada.

On January 28, 1968, Jim Morrison was visiting Las Vegas for the first time with his friend, author Robert Gover (*One Hundred Dollar Misunderstanding*, 1961). After dinner, they went to the Pussycat a Go-Go. With his long straggly hair, Morrison fit in fine with his generation, but not so with that of his elders. After several drinks, he got caught up in the music and the excitement and happily feigned smoking a marijuana joint while puffing on a regular cigarette.

That was not cool to the security guards present. One of them hit Morrison over the head with a billy club and shoved him toward the door. His head bleeding, Morrison shoved back. The police were called. No one wanted the trouble this longhaired man was causing.

Morrison and Gover were arrested. Destined to be a rock legend, on this night, Morrison was just another young man charged with public drunkenness and vagrancy. He would not spend much time in the Clark County Jail. After being fingerprinted and having mugshots taken, Morrison and Gover were bailed out by a friend. He would travel to Paris in 1970. The Pussycat a Go-Go closed for good in 1971 and the rest is rock 'n' roll history.

Cold-Blooded

Early 1959 saw ex-cons Perry Smith and Dick Hickok making plans. These did not include plans to turn their lives around but rather the implementation of a get rich scheme based on a tale they had been told while in prison. Early in the evening of November 15, they drove to the Clutter family farmhouse in Holcomb, Kansas, in search of the safe that contained more money than the pair had ever seen. It did not exist. The inmate who had whispered tall tales to them about the Clutter's wealth had lied. Angry at having gone on a fool's errand, Smith slit Mr. Clutter's throat, and then he and Hickok shot the other three members of the family in the head.

On the run, the paroled convicts stole money and cars as they traveled across the county. Eventually, they ended up in Nevada, where Perry Smith was born. Six weeks after slaughtering the Clutter family, they were arrested on December 30, 1959, in Las Vegas. Truman Capote's blockbuster *In Cold Blood* had yet to be written, so no one in Vegas paid much attention to a couple of ex-cons who had killed a family in faraway Kansas.

Smith and Hickok spent six days in the Las Vegas jail. On January 6, 1960, officers of the Kansas bureau of investigation escorted them back to Kansas to stand trial for their crimes. Both men confessed and were subsequently found guilty. While imprisoned and awaiting their executions, they were visited regularly by writer Truman Capote. They were hanged on April 14, 1965.

Divorce Is Not in the Cards

Richard Magdayo Dahan met and fell in love with Daisy while they were living in the Philippines. He was twelve years older than she was, but the age difference did not matter to either of them. After a brief romance, they moved in together. They married in 2011 and moved to Las Vegas where he worked as a chef at one of the large hotel and casinos on the strip. It all might have ended happily if not for Richard's ex-girlfriend and his children.

Daisy was jealous. She did not want him speaking to his former girlfriend. They had been married three years and Daisy asked for a divorce. It was not the first time she had asked since coming to the U.S. As he usually did, Richard Dahan ignored her divorce talk. His parents had never divorced. He did not believe in divorce and Daisy was not going to divorce him. Yet on the afternoon of January 11, 2014, she was insistent—she wanted out of the marriage. She demanded a divorce and was not about to back down this time. She raised her voice, infuriating her husband.

Richard Dahan grabbed a serrated knife and stabbed her in the neck. "No, oh Lord, no," she cried. When the knife became entangled in her hair, he struck her on the top of the head with a meat cleaver. He then stabbed her in the abdomen and as she continued to moan, he cut the corners of her mouth to silence her. He panicked. He walked around and around the kitchen before climbing into the shower fully clothed. After changing clothes, he drove to the nearest police station. "I stabbed my wife to death," he announced to the first officer he encountered.

Casino No-Nos

Skimming is a thing of the past. Back in the mob rule days of Las Vegas, skimming was ubiquitous to gaming. Part of the day's take was always reserved and set aside for mob interests, and everyone knew it. Today's run-ins with the rules are out of ignorance and not out of a desire to circumvent rules and regulations. In 2003, the Mirage paid the largest fine in Gaming Control Board history when it forked over a $5-million check to the Nevada Gaming Control Board. The Gaming Control Board has a set of rules and regulations that every gaming establishment must follow. These are standard, but several employees at the Mirage got sloppy with their record-keeping, costing them their jobs and their erstwhile bosses a large amount of money.

In 2003, management at the El Cortez went further when they permitted a casino management employee to gamble and lose and run up a tab at the casino. This just is not done for obvious reasons. The El Cortez was fined $15,000 for the two violations of state law.

Just a Kid

In July 1997, Sara Gruber was a pretty California girl from a broken home, craving adventure. She caught the eye of a pimp, who talked her into running away from home and coming to Las Vegas with him. He would love her and take care of her and in exchange she would live an exciting life, and that was what the teenage Sara was looking for—love, money, and excitement. At sixteen, she was already wise beyond her years—schooled by her pimp and smart enough to know she needed to pose as an adult in order to play in this game and make money.

So she traveled to Arizona, where she presented a fake birth certificate, so she could apply for and receive a driver's license that gave her age as twenty-one. With her make-up on and her hair styled, she could easily pass for older than sixteen. With her legitimate license, she became a legal adult by the name of Alana Alvarado. She was just another pretty young woman living it up in Las Vegas. Quaffing cocktails in casino hotels dimly lit bars, she scoped out potential customers—this one looked nice; that one did not; this one had money to spend; that one had less bills in his wallet than she did. Credit cards did not count.

As Alana, she raked in the money. Like other prostitutes, she worked most of the big-name places until someone got wise (they always did) and reported her to security. Gamblers pay the casinos' bills. Consequently, no casino wants prostitutes taking players away from the slots and the table games. Prostitutes like Alana are summarily escorted to the door and told not to return. This did not deter Alana, neither did the thirteen citations for prostitution that she had been issued during her short time in Las Vegas.

Legalized in certain areas of Nevada, prostitution is not legal in Las Vegas. Nonetheless, Alana played the game. She paid her attorney very well to keep her out of jail and continued being Alana Alvarado, prostitute. Once she saw all that quick and easy money she could make, falling into lockstep in a pair of stilettos got a whole lot easier, especially when her good-looking, glib-tongued pimp was delivering a seductive line about love and romance. Young women fall for it every day and every night.

In October, she had been in Las Vegas for two months. She was at the Luxor and looking for business. At the bar, she met Michael Joseph Hathaway, the son of a Bay Area police lieutenant, and like her, he was from Northern California. He bought her a drink and they talked. Finally, it came down to business. After some discussion, Hathaway agreed to pay Alana $300 for oral sex, and up to his room they went.

Once behind closed doors and the deal done, Hathaway wanted more. "How much for intercourse?" he asked. Alana thought quickly. That would cost him more, much more—$1,500 was her price and she told him so. This was not what Hathaway wanted to hear. He balked; he was not about to pay that much. Alana was not going to waste time arguing with him as there were plenty of other men more willing to spend their money. She grabbed her purse and moved toward the door. He angrily grabbed her from behind and held her so that she could not move. She struggled to free herself as his hands encircled her neck. His grip tightened as he began choking her.

This was the one situation she had hoped never to encounter. She begged him not to kill her. He released his hands and shoved her to the floor. She was alive and still breathing, but barely. Hathaway was not going to let her leave this room alive. He finished her off by standing, with his full weight on her windpipe for several minutes, until he was certain she was dead. Then, he sexually assaulted her.

He left Alana there in his room at the Luxor, where a hotel maid discovered her body the next morning. Except she was not Alana Alvarado—her name was Sara Gruber and she was just a kid, a sixteen-year-old kid who believed when a pimp promised her love, good-times and lots of money; a kid who fell in with a pimp who drove her to Las Vegas where she worked the streets for him until she met the wrong man.

In 1998, Michael Joseph Hathaway confessed to killing Sara Gruber and sexually assaulting her corpse. He explained to investigators that he had no idea why he killed her. He agreed to a plea bargain and was sentenced to twenty years for the crime with possibility of parole.

The rest of the story involves Pierre Hudson, the pimp who brought Sara Gruber to Las Vegas from California. When he was arrested in 1999, Hudson pleaded guilty to one count of transportation of a minor across state lines for purposes of prostitution. Hudson was sentenced to thirty-three months in prison, to be followed by three years of supervised release once he got out of prison.

"I Hear Voices"

Aside from her mother and her three-year-old son, Erline Folker had no family in Las Vegas. The pretty divorcee's father and his large family were all back in Washington, where she had been born and raised. Erline (Childers) graduated in the Walla Walla high school class of 1953, fell in love, and got married. That was typical of the early 1950s. Less so in the era of *Father Knows Best* and *Leave it to Beaver* was the divorce that left Erline alone with a young son to raise.

Hoping for a fresh start, Erline came to Las Vegas and moved in with her mother. She had no interest in working in the gaming industry, so she took a job as a stenographer at a stationery store. It paid the bills and kept them fed. The divorce had not been easy, but she was starting to date again. Life was good. Then on the afternoon of November 3, 1958, Erline Folker encountered madness.

Jack Rainsberger had been in and out of trouble since he was twelve years old. At twenty-three, that encompassed half his life. The Los Angeles handyman had no friends. Whenever he did converse with his co-workers and employers, the subject was so esoteric that he became known as a genius. Rainsberger came to Las Vegas because the voices ordered him to do so; these voices also demanded that he select a victim for his human sacrifice. He was looking for just such a victim when he glanced into the window of the stationery store and saw Erline Folker. She would be his sacrifice. He roamed around the neighborhood and waited for her to get off work.

Late in the afternoon, she covered her typewriter and tidied her desk. Telling her co-workers that she would see them tomorrow, Erline walked out the door. Rainsberger followed her to her car. He was quick. Before she realized what was happening, he pressed a knife against her back and shoved her into the car. Still holding the knife against her, he crawled into the backseat and ordered her to drive out to the desert. Erline Folker would never be seen alive again.

That night, Jack Rainsberger went to the Las Vegas Police Station and filed a robbery report. He claimed that he had been robbed and left to walk miles in the desert. The next morning, Erline's mother filed a missing person's report; her daughter had not come home all night. This was not like her. Before the police could investigate the robbery, or the missing woman's whereabouts, a bus driver discovered a body in the desert. Erline Folker's body was clad in the tweed skirt and blouse she had worn to work the day before. Her underclothes were wrapped around her neck. The woman's throat had been slit from ear to ear.

With news of the discovery of Erline Folker's body, Jack Rainsberger had a story to share. He confessed to the murder. He explained to officers that the voices had told him to find a human sacrifice:

> I saw her in the stationery store and decided she would be my victim. I followed her to her car and made her drive to the desert. Then I sacrificed her. It was all part of a regular ritual, but I can't tell you how I go through it.

Rainsberger was convicted of Folker's murder and sentenced to die. He would spend the next thirteen years of his life on Nevada's death row, waiting for (and appealing) that appointment with the gas chamber. Then, in 1972, the death penalty was brought before the Supreme Court in *Furman v. Georgia, Jackson v. Georgia*, and *Branch v. Texas* (known collectively as the landmark case *Furman v. Georgia* (408 U.S. 238)) On June 29, 1972, the court voided forty death penalty statutes, commuting the sentences of 629 death row inmates across the U.S. and suspending the death penalty.

Jack Rainsberger, who wrote poetry and created crossword puzzles, now had reason to hope that someday he might be a free man. Over the next several years, he would suffer a heart attack and attend nineteen unsuccessful parole hearings in which Erline Folker's grown son would also appear. Eventually, Rainsberger would be set free to live out his life in Reno where he died at the age of seventy-two.

The Murder of Bridget Gray

Girls from well-adjusted, mom-and-dad, and apple-pie homes rarely turn to prostitution. The others fall through the cracks. Bridget Gray was one of those girls. Her father was not in her life and her mother was not able to take care of her. Tragically, Bridget was just another throwaway kid who spent her childhood in and out of foster homes. Barely in her teens, Bridget turned to prostitution as a way to hold and keep a pimp's love. She soon learned that a pimp's love is an oxymoron. If there is any love, it is the love of money. As she got older, she tried once or twice to get off the streets and into a real job. It never worked. Sooner or later, she was back with a pimp and back on the streets.

March 3, 2006 was Bridget's twenty-second birthday. While other young women celebrated their birthdays in a myriad of ways with friends and families, Bridget was alone in one of the bars at the Mandalay Bay on the Strip.

She was hoping to turn a trick and make some money. She was an attractive young woman. Dressed in the overly seductive manner of women in her profession, Bridget absently stirred her drink and waited.

Over 6.5 million convention attendees come to Las Vegas annually; David Flansburg was one of them. After all the speeches, sales pitches, and backslapping, Flansburg was ready for some relaxation. He wandered into the bar where Bridget Gray sat nursing her drink. He stared at her as he tossed back a couple of drinks. Sizing her up as a prostitute, he walked over to her and sat down. Flansburg ordered another drink for each of them. As they made small talk, she told him that if he wanted a good time, she could provide it for a fee.

Flansburg thought about that for a moment and finished his drink. Why not? He was staying here at the Mandalay Bay, so there was no need to call a cab; a quick trip in the elevator was as far as they needed to go. He agreed to her offer, and up to his room on the twenty-fifth floor they went. When they arrived in his room, Flansburg discovered that he did not have enough money to pay her fee. Fortunately, an ATM is never far away in the gambling establishments of Las Vegas. They took the elevator down to the ATM together, and he was now flush with cash. Back in his room, they negotiated a price and Bridget was paid.

While Flansburg freshened up in the bathroom, Bridget quickly slipped out of her clothing. There would be other tricks and more money tonight. She absently glanced around the room and noticed his slacks, neatly folded across a chair. Curiosity got the better of Bridget. With her back to the bathroom door, she quickly rifled through his pants pockets. She opened his wallet and greed took over. She pulled out a few bills. There did not seem to be any harm in taking some extra money; prostitutes steal from their customers all the time. So intent with stuffing the bills in her handbag, Bridget did not hear him come from the bathroom. He was enraged at being played a fool. How dare this woman steal from him? He raced toward her.

Only then did she realize her mistake. Bridget did not get the chance to speak as he pounced on her; his hands encircled her neck, strangling her to death on her birthday. Now he had a problem—what was he going to do with a very dead woman in his room on the twenty-fifth floor? In an attempt to destroy the evidence, he flushed her dress down the toilet and stuffed her stilettos and sweater in the box springs of the mattress. Then he pulled her body out into the hallway and gently closed the door.

Anyone could have put her body there, he told himself. Out of sight, out of mind, or so he thought, until the police came calling with a whole lot of questions.

Like the three monkeys, he saw nothing, he heard nothing, and he was saying nothing. While investigators checked clues, Flansburg decided it might be a good time to beat it back home to Santa Ana, California. Once there, he tried to forget what he had done and hoped they would never catch him. However, he had not reckoned on the sophistication of large modern Vegas hotel casinos. Surveillance cameras are everywhere for the safety of guests and that of employees as well. It would be tedious work, but detectives painstakingly went through all the surveillance video for March 3. After several hours, they found what they were looking for—there on video, in clear view, were David Flansburg and the victim walking alongside each other in the hallway and in the casino. At the ATM, she stood beside him as he took money from the machine. They had him. In May 2009, Flansburg confessed to killing Bridget Gray and was found guilty of second-degree murder. He was sentenced to ten years to life in the Nevada state prison.

High Roller Sexcapade

Las Vegas's "High Roller" is one for the Guinness Book of World Records. It is only fitting that the world's tallest Ferris wheel be located in Nevada. After all, George Washington Gale Ferris, Jr., the man who invented the Ferris wheel, was from Carson City, Nevada's state capitol. Born in Galesburg, Illinois, on February 14, 1859, George Ferris, Jr., was five years old when his family moved west to the Carson Valley. As a youth, he spent time near the Cradlebaugh Ranch and its waterwheel. Years later, it would be said that this waterwheel gave young George the idea for his Ferris wheel.

The brand-new Eiffel Tower was a big hit at the International Paris Exposition of 1889. The directors of the World Columbian Exposition decided to outdo Paris—more specifically, the Eiffel Tower. They offered a challenge to U.S. engineers—a contest to see who could come up with something that would be even more extraordinary. George Ferris, Jr., won with his 264-foot Ferris wheel, which was an instant success when the exposition opened on June 21, 1893.

The High Roller is one of Las Vegas's newest attractions. It dwarfs other wheels such as London's Eye (443 feet tall) and Paris' Roue de Paris (a mere 200 feet tall). Only 9 feet taller than the Singapore Flyer, the High Roller at 550 feet tall is the world's tallest observation wheel

(Ferris wheel). Adorned with 2,000 LED lights that constantly change color, the High Roller at the LINQ is awe-inspiring from every vantage point. When the High Roller's twenty-eight glass-enclosed capsules (cabins) are at capacity, there are 1,120 people taking the thirty-minute ride. Yoga classes are available on the High Roller, and brides looking for somewhere unique to share their vows are already eyeing the High Roller. Also, apparently, was one couple looking for a new twist on the old mile-high club.

Phillip Frank Panzica met her in the afternoon on February 5, 2016, which happened to be her twenty-first birthday. He had just broken up with his fiancée and was nursing a broken heart. They had both had too much to drink when they climbed aboard empty cabin number sixteen, ready for the ride that is billed the "Happiest Half Hour" in Las Vegas. They were alone, they were young, and they were adventuresome. The alcohol kicked in. The pair decided to undress and try a little hanky-panky of the most serious sort while alone in one of the enclosed cabins. Yet there are those windows, and passengers in other cabins caught glimpses of Panzica in the nude and of the daring duo doing the dirty. Three people recorded all the action on their cell phones. George Washington Ferris, Jr., would be rolling over in his grave if he only knew.

The frisky couple had forgotten about the ubiquitous cell phone. Then too, there was that supervisor who used the intercom to tell them to stop what they were doing and put their clothes back on. The calls were ignored. They were not the first couple to enjoy an amorous adventure on the High Roller and they certainly would not be the last. In fact, the website VitalVegas.com offers eleven tips for having sex on the high roller.

Police were summoned, and when cabin number sixteen returned to the docking area, the couple was escorted to jail and charged with certain sex acts in public, which is a felony. When asked why, they explained that they were just having a good time and did not think anyone else would notice. That might be so at 5 a.m. in Podunk town, but at 3 p.m. on a bright sunny afternoon in Las Vegas, that was unlikely. They earned five minutes of fame and a hefty fine. Then they beat it back to their own homes and their own lives.

Sadly, this story does not end well for one of the adventuresome riders. A month after being arrested for his part in the High Roller sexual hijinks in Las Vegas, Panzica was driving his girlfriend home from her job at a topless bar in his hometown of Houston, Texas, when he became the victim of a car-jacking robbery and was murdered.

Necrophilia on the North Side

Las Vegas is no stranger to weirdness. Joseph Martinez is an example. On June 29, 2017, Metro officers were called to 2140 West Charleston Blvd where they found Martinez having sex with a dead woman in a flower box outside a church. Martinez explained that she had been alive when he initiated sex with her. The coroner disagreed. The homeless woman had been dead from two to four hours; Martinez insisted she had been alive when they met the night before. The dead woman's tragic story was one of drug addiction and its destruction. She had tried, but she just could not stay off drugs. She left behind her mother and her children.

Nevada does not mess around with necrophiliacs. Their sentences can be harsh, including life imprisonment. Martinez claimed he was acquainted with the woman and that he had only tried to help her. He was arrested and charged with one count of unlawful sexual penetration of a dead body.

Turning the Tables on a Serial Killer

Street prostitution is a dangerous business—everyone knows that. Yet this fact does not stop anyone from engaging in the practice as there is no faster way to make a lot of money, yet there is no faster way to become enmeshed in a very dangerous situation.

Between March 2003 and April 2006, Las Vegas prostitutes may have worked with more apprehension than usual. During that time, four Las Vegas prostitutes disappeared under eerily similar circumstances—Lindsay Marie Harris, Misty Marie Saens, Jodi Marie Brewer, and Jessica Edith Louise Foster, four young women who likely died at the hands of a vicious serial killer who stalked prostitutes. Killing young women and leaving their dismembered bodies along highways across the U.S., the murderer went undetected. Authorities were baffled with so little evidence to go on.

On July 18, 2015, karma caught up with Neal Falls in the Charleston, West Virginia, home of his intended victim Heather Saul when she fought back. As he came through the door, Neal Falls pointed a gun at her and said, "Live or die." She had no intentions of dying and picked up a rake. Stunned, he dropped his gun and tried to take the rake from her. That was a fatal mistake. The quick-thinking Saul grabbed his gun and shot him in the head.

Investigators would find four pairs of handcuffs on the dead man's body. While searching Falls's Subaru Forester, they found a serial killer's kill kit that consisted of a machete, axes, knives, a shovel, a sledgehammer, bleach, plastic trash bags, and bulletproof vests.

Suspecting that Neal Falls was a serial killer, police started matching up victims with Falls's known whereabouts during disappearances. Not surprising, he was living in Henderson, a suburb of Las Vegas, and employed at Boulder Dam (33.5 miles from Las Vegas) during the disappearance of the four Las Vegas prostitutes.

Without a doubt, Heather Saul saved her own life when she put a bullet in Neal Falls's brain. She probably saved countless other young women from the same fate as Lindsay Marie Harris, Misty Marie Saens, Jodi Marie Brewer, and Jessica Edith Louise Foster.

Trick Roll

Street prostitution is not safe for anyone. Either the prostitute or the trick (customer) can find themselves facing danger, or at least robbery. One man found this out the hard way when he encountered a known trick roll prostitute. He had become separated from his friends at the Mandalay Bay, which is easy to do in the excitement of Vegas. A pretty woman offered him a ride to the Bellagio and oral sex for a price; this was Las Vegas, and he might have heard that what happens in Las Vegas stays in Las Vegas. He should have thought about that other maxim—if it seems too good to be true, it probably is. He accepted her offer and climbed into her car, no questions asked. Yet what he did not know is that he had just hopped into the car with a woman who had her mind on one thing—robbing him.

As the car pulled away from the Mandalay, the man was eagerly pulling off his pants when he realized there were two other women in the backseat of the car. As he tried to put his pants back on, they beat and kicked him. He reached for his wallet and realized it was gone. "Give my wallet back." He demanded.

"Get the gun." One of the women yelled to the other. He did not want to die for the money and credit cards in his wallet. At the Treasure Island, the car slowed. He leapt out and tried to run away while one of the women shot at him. Luckily, he got away with his life. Police caught up with the trick roll team and arrested them. They may be off the streets for a while, but there will always be others to take their place.

Teenage Trick Roll

The scene of the crime was the Uptown Motel at 813 Ogden Avenue in downtown Las Vegas. That was 2002. A modern luxury apartment building stands in its stead today.

Alisha Burns was fifteen and cute. Her boyfriend, Steve Kaczmarek, was thirty-three years old. She was a ward of the court and in foster care in Ohio when they met and fell in love. Together, they stole her foster parents' car and drove to Las Vegas. Yet the city was not all bright lights, showgirls, and easy money; it was harder than they had imagined. After their money ran out, they ended up living on the streets. Alisha panhandled for cash and pretended to be a prostitute. This is when they met Pedro Villareal at a fast food restaurant and he offered Alisha $200 for sex; this is also where the story shows that no good deed goes unpunished.

On September 25, 2002, Alisha and Kaczmarek showed up at Villareal's apartment pretending that Alisha was here to collect that $200 for services rendered. Villareal eagerly opened the door for them, unaware that they had come here with some very bad intentions. Money made their world go round and whatever Villareal had, they were going to take—by force if necessary.

Villareal worked in a casino kitchen and his wages and his meager possessions were far from princely. Whatever he had, it was a hell of a lot more than either Alisha or Kaczmarek had. Once inside the small apartment, Kaczmarek hit Villareal, knocking him out. They tied his hands and feet up with electrical cords, stuffed a sock in his mouth, threw a pillowcase over his head, and dragged him to the bathroom where they tossed him into the bathtub. The shower head was left running. When their victim did not die fast enough, Alisha finished him off by jumping up and down on his neck.

Their take was a gold bracelet, a video cassette recorder (VCR), and $40 in cash. They pawned the dead man's belongings and might have gotten away with the murder if not for Steve Kaczmarek's jailhouse braggadocio. While in jail on another unrelated charge, he boasted of the murder to not one inmate, but two. They snitched and detectives came calling. Kaczmarek told it all.

After being arrested, Alisha took a deal. She pleaded guilty to one count of second-degree murder and the prosecution dropped robbery and kidnapping charges. She was sentenced to ten years to life imprisonment with the possibility of parole. At fifteen, she became the youngest inmate ever incarcerated at the Florence McClure Women's Correctional Center in Las Vegas.

Steven Kaczmarek was not so lucky. He was found guilty of first-degree murder, robbery, and kidnapping and was sentenced to death. He appealed and was offered a deal to drop the appeal in exchange for life without the possibility of parole. He took the deal.

Harry Wham and the Keyboard Lounge Murder

Harry Wham was a pioneering scuba diver. He served during World War II as a member of the Navy's elite underwater demolition team, whose job was to make amphibian landings safe by finding and destroying enemy (and natural) obstacles. Harry loved the water. After the war, he lived in Southern California so that he could indulge his love of diving. A few of his diving buddies were surprised when he moved to Las Vegas as there were not much diving opportunities in the desert. Yet Harry followed his dream and founded the Whamco Divers.

His business card from this time offers instruction, underwater photography, diving equipment, and salvage. The dive location of choice (actually the only diving location nearby) was Lake Mead, the 247-sq. mile manmade lake roughly 94 miles from Las Vegas.

Harry Wham was a man of many talents. In addition to his diving business, he was also a pianist, and a damn good one at that. In the late 1950s into the early 1960s, he and his wife, Toni, along with singer, Peggy Dietrick, entertained patrons in the Gay 90s Lounge at the Silver Slipper.

By 1983, he had met and married his last wife, Peggy, and bought the Keyboard Lounge. The new Mrs. Wham was a singer who went by the name of "Stormy" and happened to be twenty years younger than her husband was. Harry knew that Stormy had a daughter and a volatile temper. What he did not know was that Stormy had a lover on the side. Before long, all she wanted from Harry was his money and the full ownership of the lounge.

The subject of Harry's demise, and how to hasten it, was fodder for kitchen table conversation whenever Harry was nowhere around. Stormy, her lover, her daughter, and her daughter's lover (who happened to be the brother of Stormy's lover) finally settled upon a plan. She would hire hitman John Oliver Snow to kill Harry. In order to finance the hit, Stormy stole money from the safe at the Keyboard Lounge.

So there was Harry at the Keyboard Lounge, taking requests and tickling the ivories, totally unaware that the missus had paid one John Snow $5,000 dollars to make her a widow. Yet the hit did not happen that night at the Keyboard Lounge. Ignorance is probably bliss. The killer did not succeed in his first attempt at killing Harry, so another plot was hastily devised.

On February 13, 1983, Stormy gave her daughter the keys to the Wham garage. The daughter was to give them to Snow when she picked him up at his motel. Hidden in the garage, he would lie in wait for his chance to finish the job. He waited until Harry Wham came into the garage before pumping several bullets into him. Alas, Stormy was a widow and entitled to everything. She was also free to be with her lover. However, police detectives are not stupid.

It did not take them long to determine that Harry's murder was not some robbery gone wrong. They suspected Stormy and her rotten disposition immediately. They needed proof, but no one was talking. Then, Stormy's sister mentioned to a friend what she knew about the murder. When pushed to go to the police, she refused to turn on her sister. So the friend stepped forward to tell what he had been told; it was enough to send them all to the penitentiary. He agreed to wear a wire next time he talked with Stormy's sister.

The recording was the evidence investigators needed to arrest Stormy and her cohorts. Snow was given the death penalty. Stormy, her lover, her daughter, and her daughter's lover were all given life without the possibility of parole. The daughter was paroled in 1986. The brothers have since died.

On December 2, 1998, Peggy Stormy Wham was released from prison— not because she had beaten the system, but because at fifty-six, she was a wasted old woman dying from the ravages of pancreatic and stomach cancer. She weighed just 80 lb. According to her attorney, Stormy's stomach and her pancreas had been removed. Her esophagus was attached to her colon; she could not hold down food and needed to be fed six times a day; it is doubtful any of Harry Wham's fans were crying a river over her prognosis. Thirteen years later, John Oliver Snow appealed his death sentence in July 2011 and was turned down.

Love

The Paet family lived in a desert modern stucco house on Alta Monte Court in Mountain Edge. Both Nathan and Michelle Paet liked the fresh new neighborhood of southwestern style homes in Mountain Edge, a master community in southwest Las Vegas. It was the ideal place to raise their four kids. Nathan and Michelle had been high school sweethearts in Guam and had been married four years. They were a happy couple, and then Michelle met Michael Rudolph Rodriguez.

It was a workplace romance. Michelle Paet and Rodriguez met as co-workers and were immediately attracted to each other. The relationship quickly evolved from flirtation to a sexual affair. They wanted to be together forever, but Michelle Paet was not about to simply walk away from her marriage. She wanted to live in style, so she and Michael Rudolph Rodriguez needed to take her husband's $650,000 insurance money with them when they rode off into the sunset. Before that could happen, her husband would first have to die.

By October, the lovebirds had been involved with each other for four months and had begun plotting the murder of Nathan Paet in earnest. Rodriguez enlisted the aid of two friends who would help with the plan. On the night of December 1, 2010, they were all set, ready to carry out their plot to murder Nathan Paet.

Staff Sgt. Nathan Paet had been assigned to the 757th Aircraft Maintenance Squadron at nearby Nellis Air Force Base for the past three years. The Iraq War veteran had a reputation of being punctual. He did not like to be late for work ever. On Wednesday night, he was behind schedule. He hurriedly dressed and dashed through the house. It was 11.30 p.m.; he worked the graveyard shift to make more money for the family. He had gotten used to working through the night, but that night, he was scrambling to get to work on time. "I'm gonna be late," he said to no one in particular. "I'm gonna be late."

He kissed his kids and went into the master bedroom to say goodbye to his wife. As he bent over the bed to kiss her, Michelle put her cell phone down and raised her cheek to receive his kiss. When he had gone, she picked up her phone. Chuckling, she texted to her lover Michael Rudolph Rodriguez, "He's rushing to get out the door, LOL."

Out in the garage, Nathan Paet lifted the door. He had done it a dozen times, though this time would be different. A black Cadillac was parked across the street. Two men—Michael Rudolph Rodriguez and his accomplice—lay in wait for Paet. When they saw him, Rodriguez jumped out of the Cadillac, ran up to the unsuspecting Paet, and shot him five times. Shocked, Paet stumbled back into his home and collapsed there, bleeding to death in front of his wife and his four children. Michelle Paet called 911. Nathan Paet was rushed to University Medical Center, but it was already too late. Hours after her husband's death, Michelle Paet texted a smiley face to Rodriguez.

Within the week, police arrested Rodriguez and the two accomplices who had aided in the plot to kill Paet and collect his life insurance. Rodriguez claimed to have been in bed with an "ex-porn star" at the time of the killing. The woman would later tell that he had offered her $5,000 for an alibi. When this story blew up in his face, Rodriguez talked. Michelle Paet was arrested next. With the death penalty on the table for each of them, all that sexual desire went out the window. Charged with murder, it was every man for himself. There would be no long, drawn-out trial. In order to avoid the death penalty, Rodriguez made a deal and pleaded guilty to Nathan Paet's murder. In the deal, he would give up his right to appeal and was sentenced to life imprisonment without parole. Michelle Paet took a similar deal, pleading guilty to conspiracy to commit murder and first-degree murder with use of a deadly weapon.

She, too, will spend the rest of her life behind bars without opportunity for parole.

The DuPont Murder Case

In 1953, DuPont family fortune heiress, Lisa Dean, was a young woman of privilege and wealth. She was also used to getting her own way, which included marrying E. Haring "Red" Chandor. The marriage produced two sons and was happy for a time. Then, Lisa fell in love with her gynecologist, Dr. John MacGuigan. It did not take long for "Red" to figure out what was going on between his wife and the man who had delivered his two sons. He sued for divorce on the grounds of adultery. Once the Chandor marriage was asunder, Lisa married the good doctor. The union was a happy one, right up to 1985 when Dr. MacGuigan died of a heart attack, making Lisa a widow.

Three years later, Lisa advertised for a groundskeeper, which is when Christopher Moseley entered her life. She was older than him by eleven years; that and a big fat bank account separated them. Nonetheless, romance blossomed right along with the flower garden. Moseley and Lisa Dean Chandor MacGuigan were married the following year. As the newlyweds settled into wedded bliss in the Delaware mansion, Lisa lost a son to a heroin overdose and her other son, Dean, fell in love with Pati Margello, a woman who, like himself, was a drug addict with AIDS.

Lisa did not approve of the romance. Dean carried the DuPont pedigree, and Pati was beneath him. Besides, he already had a wife, but lucky for Dean and Pati, the wife wanted no part of him and moved out of the home. Not so lucky was the fact that Lisa was paying the rent, and in an attempt to get her son to dump Pati, Lisa stopped paying the rent. The plan failed. Dean and the penniless Pati had no choice; they moved out.

When Dean went to Las Vegas in 1998 to establish residency for his divorce from his wife, Pati went too. Although his mother and his stepfather tried, no amount of cajoling or money could make him turn his back on Pati. However, Mosely had a plan. While playing the big shot at a local casino he met Diana Hironaga, a streetwise former porn star turned prostitute, who was down on her luck. As Kiane Lee, Hironaga had performed in more than sixteen pornographic films. Yet she was on the wrong side of forty and time was catching up with her. Then, she sat down at a poker machine and met Christopher Moseley, who was throwing money around the casino like it really did grow on the palm trees that line most every street in Las Vegas. They talked, and while they did so, he continually fed $100 bills into her machine. She was impressed.

Moseley had a problem named Pati. Hironaga needed money and her next fix, but he had a solution. He gave Hironaga $5,000 to convince Pati to get off drugs, break up with Dean, and leave town. The plan failed. Now, there was no choice. Another plan was put into operation—Pati must die. So Moseley gave Hironaga $5,000 to enlist Ricardo Murillo and Joseph Balignasa for the purpose of killing Pati. For their handiwork, they would get $5,000 each as well.

Hironaga convinced Pati that there were two high rollers waiting for them in room six at the Del Mar Resort motel on Las Vegas Blvd. Ever in need of cash, Pati agreed to meet the two men posing as tricks. She must have wondered why high rollers would choose the Del Mar and not a classier hotel. Something made her realize that these men were not what they pretended to be. Sensing a trap, she called Dean for help, begging him to come and get her. High on drugs, he unwittingly abandoned her to her fate by ignoring her plight and falling asleep. Hironaga held her down while Murillo slipped Balignasa's belt around her neck and choked the life from her. The killers then wrapped her body in plastic and stuffed it in the air-conditioning vent.

When she did not return home the next day, Dean called the police. Her body was discovered the following day, and room registration led back to Diana Hironaga, who quickly confessed. In exchange for a reduced sentence, both she and Christopher Moseley talked. Diana Hironaga was paroled. Dean MacGuigan died in 2013.

Nightmare at a Dream House

The house is still there on Versailles Court in Henderson. The $1-million plus home offers a sparkling blue swimming pool in the backyard and is surrounded by lush greenery and squat palms. A serene house, it hardly seems a place where such horror would ever have been played out. Yet, one night in early October 1996, tragedy came calling.

Judith Smith could not have been happier with her dream home. The palatial home her husband Joe rented for them was located within an upscale gated community in Henderson. She could not wait to furnish and decorate her new home. Eventually, Joe promised, to buy them one as nice or nicer, but Judith loved this home. So Joe struck a deal with the landlord to purchase it from him.

Ecstatic, she believed the home would soon be hers. She had no idea that her husband was a con man who had spent some time in jail. Her daughters from a previous marriage, Kristy Gaye Cox and Wendy Jean Cox, moved in with the Smiths and were almost as excited about the home as Judith was. At twenty, Wendy Jean had other things on her mind. She was in love. The young woman was engaged and set to begin her own matrimonial adventure within the month.

Joe was fifty; the pressure to pay the bills and maintain the lavish lifestyle for his wife and step-children overwhelmed him. Knowing full well he did not have the money, he promised a check to the landlord to seal the deal that would make the house his and Judith's.

By October 5, 1996, he had created such a financial mess. There was no way out. They all had to die, and he did the unthinkable. One by one, Joseph Weldon Smith killed his family; his wife Judith and his step-daughters Kristy and Wendy were bludgeoned with a claw hammer and strangled to death in their beautiful dream house. He left them where he had killed them.

When the landlord arrived the next day to get the check Smith had promised him, he was attacked by Smith. As he ran from room to room in the 5,000-sq. foot home, he discovered the bodies of Judith Smith and her daughters. Fearing for his life, he dove through a window and ran to safety.

It would be six months before the law caught up with Smith. He had been hiding out at a motel in Inglewood, California. He stood trial and was convicted of the three murders. He received the death penalty for the murder of Kristy and Wendy.

Mobsters

> *A sharp 10-year-old boy could have come to the conclusion that crime and politics in this state are on friendly terms.*
>
> Hank Greenspun, Las Vegas Sun editor

In this assessment, Greenspun was probably spot on—it was doubtful the mob could have gotten such a stronghold in Las Vegas without being on friendly terms with several politicians and a few officers of the law.

The mob discovered the potential of Las Vegas long before legit corporations realized just how much money there was to be had in legalized gambling. In March 1931, Nevada finally made gaming legal. The only state to do so, Nevada upped the ante by offering quickie marriages and divorces as well. A six-week residency was all the time needed to obtain a divorce. Scandalous to the rest of the nation, the divorce laws alone drew countless women and men to the Silver State. Most of them went to Reno for a six-week residency and a divorce. Ria Langham changed all that when she decided on Las Vegas as the place to divorce her errant movie star husband Clark Gable in 1939. Las Vegas was closer to Hollywood than Reno, and other stars soon followed.

The mob was watching. Divorce did not interest them. The mob is all about the money; legalized gambling was where the money was. It certainly interested them. Here was the perfect money laundering opportunity.

Benjamin Bugsy Siegel

Hollywood restaurateur, publisher of the *Hollywood Reporter*, and gambler Billy Wilkerson kept busy watching his Las Vegas dream take shape in the form of a highbrow gambling establishment. Wilkerson ran a swanky restaurant in Hollywood and liked rubbing elbows with film stars and mobsters. He had the idea of enticing Hollywood's elite to Las Vegas with fine dining and games of chance. All he had to do was build a classy enough place and they would travel that 200 miles across the desert.

Like Wilkerson, Siegel admired class. He was impressed with what he saw and although he already owned a percentage of the El Cortez downtown, he wanted what Wilkerson had. In this, luck was on Bugsy's side. Wilkerson ran out of money. A loan from the mob is the kiss of death for any business owner hoping to remain independent, and in true mob fashion, Bugsy came to the rescue with a check and muscled Wilkerson out of his dream and into an agreement. A legal document was drawn up and Wilkerson walked away from his dream.

No other city in the United States has a memorial dedicated to a mobster, but Las Vegas does. The Bugsy Siegel memorial is in the garden courtyard near the wedding chapel at the Flamingo Las Vegas Hotel Casino. I suppose you could say it is the Flamingo's homage to the casino hotel's first owner. Benjamin "Bugsy" Siegel is often been called "the Father of Las Vegas." Others were here long before he was; nonetheless, he is credited with being the first to see the potential here in the desert. While that is not quite true, antics of the handsome Bugsy gave way to legend.

Bugsy Siegel was sent west in 1939 to look after the mob's interest in Los Angeles, particularly the race wire that transmitted results of horse races to local bookies. While overseeing his bosses' interests, Bugsy occasionally headed for a little rest and relaxation in the desert gambling town of Las Vegas, some 200 miles east. Gambling was new. It had only been legalized in Nevada a few years. Bugsy watched the action, intrigued with how much of their money gamblers were willing to risk at the tables, the roulette wheels, and the slots. He may have only had an eighth-grade education, but Bugsy was smart enough to figure the odds.

There was a tremendous amount of money to be made, and amazingly, it was all legal. The suckers could not wait to hand over their cash. They might have called it gambling, but Bugsy knew better. He was no one's fool; the odds are always in the house's favor. Sooner or later, the house always wins.

There were a few gambling establishments like the El Rancho and the Last Frontier, but Las Vegas still lagged behind Reno as a glamourous nightlife and gambling fun spot. The forty-year-old city had seen its shot at fame come and go with the Boulder Dam Project. Hollywood hotshots still preferred Reno. Las Vegas needed new direction. With his ego in overdrive, Benjamin Siegel realized he was just the man to see that it happened.

Siegel called the hotel "the Flamingo." There are many stories as to how Siegel arrived at that name. According to one, he chose this name in honor of his long-legged girlfriend Virginia Hill who had a penchant for colorful flamboyant attire. Another story claims the name stems from his admiration for the flamingos at the Hialeah Park racetrack. Regardless of why and how he named the Flamingo, the name has endured; in a town of constant flux, that is more than can be said for most Las Vegas casino hotels.

Under Bugsy's watchful eye, work on the Flamingo continued while his bosses back east anxiously watched the bottom line, waiting for his gamble to pay off. Not everyone was happy with the project. On August 1, 1946, *The Las Vegas Tribune* carried a front-page editorial criticizing Bugsy for using scarce material in the building of a casino. According to the editorial, this material could be put to better use by building homes for returning war veterans, especially since the Civilian Production Administration (CPA) was organized for the purpose of building homes rather than commercial establishments. However, Bugsy was used to bending the rules when it suited him. Through bribery or not, he had obtained his building permits from the Civilian Production Administration and that was that; construction continued.

Bugsy was unaware that his bosses were being ripped off. Anything that could be obtained was generally overpriced, and then there were the delays and the thefts. One longtime Las Vegas rumor has workers stealing material from the building site in the evening only to redeliver and recharge for it the following day. Bugsy, who would eventually pay with his life for the cost overruns, was none the wiser.

Another rumor has Virginia and Bugsy stealing from his bosses in order to finance their lavish lifestyle, and this, according to rumor, is the real reason that Bugsy was killed. These thefts might have been overlooked if the Flamingo had been a success from its beginning, but it was not. Opening night in December 1946 was a catastrophe.

After $5 million, the Flamingo opened during a freak storm that was pounding the west coast. As heavy wind-driven rain washed across the valley, Jimmy Durante, Rose Marie, and other top name celebrities tried their best to entertain the sparse crowd of curious gamblers.

The Flamingo had billed itself as "the World's Greatest Resort," but the hotel was not yet ready for guests. This oversight would cost plenty. Eventually, casino customers grew tired of gambling, and when they did, they had no choice but to leave the premises, taking their money with them. This only made Bugsy's bosses even angrier with him. They had squandered enough money out here in the Nevada desert. The Flamingo was looking like one big flop.

Eventually, Bugsy would be proven right; the Flamingo would be a financial success. Unfortunately, he would be long dead when that happened. That night, he was on a crash course with destiny, and no one could save him, not even his lifelong friend Meyer Lansky.

Bugsy had controlled the race wire in California, Nevada, and Arizona. This helped to build and maintain the mob's power. Only those the mob favored would have access to the race wire. There was no way gambling establishment could take bets on races without having quick access to the race results. Yet two years after Bugsy's murder, Nevada Governor Vail Pittman took some of the mob's power away when he signed new gambling laws that put the race wire within every licensed casino's reach, for a fee of course.

Up Next—Gus Greenbaum

It is the number one rule in "mobdom"—do not steal from the boss or waste his money as the mob takes a dim view when its money is stolen or wasted. Friendship, family ties, and length of service are nothing in comparison to the bottom line, which is really the only thing that matters. Bugsy learned this lesson too late. Six months after the Flamingo's disastrous opening, he was murdered. The hit came on June 20, 1947, in Virginia Hill's Beverly Hills mansion. He was there without Hill, who had conveniently packed up and left town. For some reason, he felt safer in Beverly Hills than in Las Vegas and had not taken the same precautions there that he had in Las Vegas. His penthouse at the Flamingo was locked behind a steel-reinforced door, the windows were bulletproof, and in the closet was a special secret ladder escape that would take him to an awaiting getaway car in the garage tunnel that could lead him to safety in the eventuality that anything happened.

Bugsy Siegel's bullet-ridden body had not even been toe-tagged when Gus Greenbaum took the reins of the fabulous Flamingo; Bugsy Siegel, or what was left of him, was cooling off at the county morgue, but his dream was alive and well. Greenbaum would see that the mob's interests were protected. With Greenbaum, the mob had finally gotten it right. He did not have Bugsy's good looks and suave manner; where Bugsy was quick to anger, Gus was even-tempered and well-liked. Also, he quickly pulled the failing casino back into the black, and while he did so, Greenbaum was making the bosses some real money.

In 1955, the Flamingo was sold at a large profit. That same year, on April 20, the Rivera opened on the strip to much fanfare with flamboyant showman Liberace cutting the ribbon. He was also the Riviera's first resident entertainer. The ninth hotel casino resort to open in Las Vegas, the Riviera was unlike any of the others.

At nine stories tall, the Riviera was known as Las Vegas's first high rise, and the crowds came. Yet three months after its gala opening, the Riviera was in deep financial trouble; management was in over its head and a new team was needed. Gus had done so well with the Flamingo that his bosses tapped him to take over management of the Riviera.

He did not want any part of it. Phoenix, Arizona, was his home. He had lived there since being sent by the mob in the late 1920s. All he wanted to do now was go home to Arizona, retire, soak up some sun, and play golf; he had earned this much, he reasoned. Gus had a change of heart when his sister-in-law was murdered in what appeared to be a message from the mob—do as you are told, or you will be next—so he took over management at the Riviera. In doing so, Gus Greenbaum soon became so popular that he was affectionately known as "the Mayor of Paradise." This moniker was in reference to the fact that the strip is actually in the unincorporated town of Paradise and not Las Vegas.

While Gus oversaw the mob's interests, his wife stayed behind in Phoenix and maintained the family home at 1115 Monte Vista in the Encanto neighborhood. Although he visited often, Gus was beginning to enjoy the power he held in Vegas too much, and like Bugsy, he was a womanizer albeit not on such a grand scale. Yet Gus went further in the downward spiral of excess. He started using drugs, getting hooked on heroin, and was drinking heavily, and that was a problem. He was not doing the job the mob was paying him to do. He was skimming from the bosses to cover the expensive lifestyle he had created for himself, which was not a smart idea. However, Gus was luckier than Bugsy had been as he was given a chance. The mob sent Johnny Rosselli to make him an offer; his thefts would be forgiven if he would sell his shares to them and immediately leave town. In a lapse of memory, Gus forgot Bugsy's fate. He stupidly refused the mob's offer, making him a problem that needed to be dealt with.

Like Bugsy before him, Gus was approximately 285 miles from Vegas when "*finis*" was written on his gaming career. He was safe and sound in his home. It was three weeks before Christmas, not that anyone would know the difference in a place like Phoenix. His back had been bothering him, so he had climbed into bed and nestled against a heating pad in the large master bedroom. Gus may have dozed off or he may have looked up startled as the killers came into the room. It happened so fast he did not have time to grab his gun from the nightstand. The killers were adept with the butcher's knife; Gus's throat was cut so deeply that he was nearly decapitated. Bess Greenbaum, being in the wrong place at the wrong time, suffered much the same fate as her husband. She was battered unconscious with a large bottle and then she too suffered a slit throat. The message was clear—do not steal from the bosses, and if you do and they should offer you a second chance, by all means take it.

The housekeeper discovered the bodies of Gus and Bess the next afternoon. The shaken woman could provide no leads other than telling them how nice the Greenbaums were to work for and how Mrs. Greenbaum had driven her home the previous night.

Back in Las Vegas, the Riviera would be closed eight hours on the day of the Greenbaums funeral. That was the highest honor one could expect from a casino hotel. Among the 300 mourners at the Greenbaum memorial was Arizona Senator Barry Goldwater, who would run for president in 1964. Gus and Goldwater had been friends for quite some time. Whenever the Goldwaters were in Las Vegas, Gus played host at the Riviera. Pallbearers for Gus and Bess included some of the top bosses from both the Flamingo and the Riviera. An investigation ensued. A large reward was offered for information, but no one talked, and unsurprisingly, no one was ever charged with the murders.

Johnny Rosselli

Rosselli was yet another mobster who ended up miles from Las Vegas when the end came. Actually, Rosselli's corpse was discovered clear across the country in a 55-gallon drum in the ocean. Several years before Rosselli made contact with that drum, he was making sure the mob kept its connections in Hollywood. By the mid-1950s, he was relocated to Las Vegas, the overseer ensuring that the mob got its cut of all the money the casinos were raking in. At the same time, Roselli was a movie producer for Monogram Studios in Hollywood. The distance between the two cities is roughly 200 miles, so this does not seem all that impossible even in the 1950s.

In 1963, singer and mob pal Frank Sinatra sponsored Rosselli for membership in the exclusive Los Angeles Friars Club. This was a mistake on Frankie's part. The Friars Club was pulled into a card cheating scandal it never recovered from in part because of Rosselli's membership; this surely earned Johnny Rosselli some enemies.

Yet they were not as deadly as the enemies he gained in 1975 when he testified on Operation Mongoose, the CIA plot to assassinate Fidel Castro before the U.S. Senate Select Committee on Intelligence. Sam Giancana was also scheduled to testify. However, a hitman put a stop to Giancana's testimony, though Rosselli kept on talking.

In 1970, Rosselli was sent to prison for eleven months. Before going, he informed on the mob and how they had concealed their interest in the Frontier Hotel. Johnny Rosselli testified about the Kennedy assassination on April 23, 1976. When called back in July of that year Rosselli was nowhere to be seen. As no one ducks out on federal testimony, the FBI started an investigation. Rosselli had an airtight excuse—his decomposing body was stuffed into a 55-gallon shipping drum and floating in Dumfoundling Bay near Miami, Florida. It was generally assumed that Rosselli was killed by mobsters because he had talked once too many times, and worse, he had had the audacity to cheat them out of their Las Vegas take.

Bye-Bye Fat Herbie

There was an unwritten rule in Las Vegas that mobsters, for the most part, obeyed. Bugsy Siegel, Gus Greenbaum, and Tony Spilotro knew and understood that when it was time for a mobster to go, the deed was done elsewhere. No one wanted mobsters killing each other within the city limits. This brought a lot of heat and scared the tourists, which was very bad for business.

There have been some exceptions. Fat Herbie Blitzstein's murder was one. When he was released from prison in 1971, Blitzstein packed up and moved to Las Vegas. His longtime friend Tony Spilotro was sure to have work for him. In addition to helping the Spilotro brothers (Tony and Michael) in their Gold Rush jewelry store, Blitzstein served as Spilotro's right-hand man and bodyguard. It was Fat Herbie who went into the cash room of casinos to skim the mob's take. Former security guards still remember escorting him into the cash room with an empty satchel. Minutes later, he exited, the satchel full of loot. Due to the power Tony Spilotro wielded, Fat Herbie was well connected.

Merchandise is necessary to any retail business. To help the Gold Rush jewelry store gather merchandise more quickly, Tony Spilotro assembled a team of thieves. Their job was to burglarize wealthy Las Vegas homes for jewels, coins, and other such valuables. They avoided security alarms by punching holes in the walls of their targets, hence the name "The Hole in the Wall Gang." For a while, it was a lucrative endeavor. Wholesale is great; free is even better. Imagine how much money can pile up if goods do not have to be paid for; the Spilotro brothers did and they were flush. This also helped Blitzstein's bottom line. Yet nothing lasts forever, especially in Las Vegas.

It all came crashing down in 1983 when the Spilotro brothers and Blitzstein were arrested and charged with more crimes than there was legit jewelry at the Gold Rush. The Spilotro brothers were confident of the legal brilliance of future Las Vegas mayor Oscar Goodman, who had successfully defended a long list of crime figures. Blitzstein was not so fortunate; he was sentenced to eight years in federal penitentiary.

On second thought, it did not work out so well for the Spilotro brothers after all. They were summoned to a house in Illinois on the pretext of a mob meeting. There they were beaten nearly to death and buried alive in an Enos, Indiana, cornfield on June 14, 1986. The mob does not keep disciplinary notes in HR jackets; the mob plays for keeps.

By 1991, the old days were long gone. Fat Herbie's days of strolling in and out of cashier cages with impunity were over. His name was placed in Nevada gaming's "Black Book." He was not permitted in any gambling establishments; just to walk through the door meant being charged with a felony. In 1997, Blitzstein was sixty-two years old and living with the results of the high life and of having been a heavy smoker. A sick old man with a bad heart, he had not entirely cleaned up his act. He made his living in a repair shop on Fremont, selling used cars, running prostitution, committing insurance fraud, and loan-sharking. Any power he may have held as Spilotro's right-hand man and feared mob enforcer was a thing of the past—he was not a threat to anyone, and no one respected him. Unfortunately for Herbie, he had "friends" who wanted to take over his small-time rackets. Although it was not a big money-maker, they wanted what Herbie had. In order for them to achieve this, they would have to get rid of Fat Herbie; his friends talked it over and a deal was struck.

On January 6, 1997, Fat Herbie had been back from his vacation in Mexico for only three days. He might have been feeling pretty good when he walked into his Las Vegas townhome on Mount Vernon Ave. Whatever he was feeling, his mood shifted when he found two men waiting for him. He had lived by mob rules too long not to realize that this was the end of the road for him.

They had come earlier in the day and robbed him of all his valuables: his diamonds, Rolexes, and his cash; Fat Herbie put his hands to his head and asked, "Why me?' In response, one of the men pointed his pistol and took aim.

Seven men were eventually arrested for the slaying of Herbie Blitzstein. The most prominent of them, Peter Vincent Caruso, died of heart failure on January 10, 1999, while awaiting trial. He was fifty-nine years old. Of the other men, four pleaded guilty to lesser charges and two were acquitted.

Where's Jimmy Hoffa?

Of all the places Jimmy Hoffa's body is said to be, Las Vegas is not one of them, but Hoffa was deep in the pocket of the mob and thus was no stranger to the mob's Las Vegas connections. From 1957 to 1971, James (Jimmy) Riddle Hoffa was the undisputed leader of the powerful International Brotherhood of Teamsters Union. During his leadership, the union grew to over 2 million members strong. In 1964, Hoffa was convicted of fraud for his illegal use of the $700 million union pension funds that he had arranged as loans to mob figures. Through his connections with his attorney Morris Shenker, much of that money went to the building and or expansions of Las Vegas casinos; that is where Hoffa's power was—he controlled the purse strings.

After three years of unsuccessful appeals, Hoffa was sent to Lewisburg Federal Penitentiary in Pennsylvania in March 1967. He was in good company as the inmate list of Lewisburg reads as a "Who's Who" of organized crime. Hoffa missed hitman Whitey Bulger, who had been released from Lewisburg two years earlier.

Two days before Christmas 1971, Hoffa received a wonderful Christmas present from President Richard ("Tricky Dick") Nixon—he was notified that he had received a presidential pardon and his thirteen-year sentence was commuted to time served. Therefore, after nearly five years, he was a free man. There was talk of a back-room deal and a $1 million payoff to Nixon. There was also speculation as to why the Democrat-leaning Teamsters endorsed the Republican Nixon for re-election rather than the Democrat George McGovern that election cycle.

Yet that is politics and mobsters for you. Jimmy Hoffa was released and was anxious to resume leadership of the teamsters. However, things had changed in those five years. Before being incarcerated, Hoffa had appointed Frank Fitzsimmons as union president. The mob favored Fitzsimmons, who ran the union until his 1981 death. Whatever he may have thought, Hoffa was not returning to his old position as he had outlived his usefulness. The Flamingo, the Stardust, Aladdin, Circus Circus, the Desert Inn, the Dunes, the Riveria, the Sands, and the Tropicana were mobbed up and happy.

On July 30, 1975, Jimmy Hoffa kissed his wife goodbye and drove toward what he thought was a business lunch meeting. No one has seen or heard from Hoffa since then. Every few years, the FBI receives a credible tip and a search is conducted for the missing and presumed dead Hoffa. He was declared dead in 1982 and would be over a hundred years old if alive, so odds are it is more than presumption. There are more theories as to who killed him and where his body might be than there are slot machines in Las Vegas—according to Google, there are about 197,000, and that is a lot. Hoffa probably vanished because he got in the way and stood between the mob and the Teamsters' money.

Out in the Desert

According to Las Vegas legend, the desert outside the city holds a lot of secrets and just as many bodies. The arid climate makes it the perfect spot for a body dump. Some of those bodies are never discovered as the coyotes and other foraging animals see to that. The bodies that are found may never be identified. The body of Al Bramlet fit neither category.

In the casino industry there is a saying, "The higher up you go, the closer to the door you get." It is a reminder of the fallacy that being a boss means job security. Apparently, this can be applied to union leadership as well.

Al Bramlet came to Las Vegas in 1946. For the next thirty years, he singlehandedly helped the Culinary Workers Local 226 to grow and to become a force to reckon with. Under his leadership, it grew from 1,500 members to 22,000. Bramlet was one of the most powerful men in Nevada.

On February 24, 1977, secretary-treasurer of Las Vegas Culinary Workers Local 226 and president of the Nevada AFL-CIO, Al Bramlet was returning from a union business trip to Reno where he had tried to settle a union squabble. His plane touched down at McCarran International Airport around 3 p.m.—on time. He disembarked the plane, and then he vanished.

A year earlier, Bramlet had angered casino owners when he successfully crippled several casinos with a strike that lasted fifteen days and closed down the strip. Management was not overly fond of him, but he was popular with union members. He treated those who worked their asses off in the casino service industry with a respect that management often withheld. Al could talk the talk. He was one of them, although he wore more expensive clothes and jewelry, drove a nicer car, and lived in a higher-class neighborhood than most of them ever would; this was thanks in part to his mob connections.

He might have politely asked his server to refill his coffee cup and left a generous toke when he finished his meal, but not everyone liked Al. He had some powerful enemies. In its March 14, 1977 issue, *Time Magazine* said Bramlet "made enemies as easily as gamblers throw dice."

The sharp-dressing sixty-year-old's worried wife of two months was frantic. It was not like her husband not to call home and let her know when he was going to be late. Sensing that something must be wrong, she contacted the F.B.I. for help in locating him. Mrs. Bramlet was not alone in her concern. The 22,000-member Culinary Union also wanted answers. Bramlet's assistant, Ben Schmoutey, announced a $25,000 reward for information on his whereabouts.

On March 17, St. Patrick's Day, they found Bramlet. His bullet-ridden nude body was discovered by rock hounds in a shallow grave near Mt. Potosi in the desert southwest of Las Vegas. Bramlet had been shot in the head. Apparently, he had brought too much attention to himself and thus caused problems for the underworld and its involvement in the union. Al Bramlet had to be taken care of.

An informant who had intimate knowledge of the murder had already come forward. Eugene Vaughn told a sad sordid story. He was with the two killers when they picked up Bramlet at the airport and drove him to the desert; after offering him a drink of whiskey, they shot and killed him. Investigators were not surprised to learn that the father–son hitman team of Tom and Gramby Hanley was responsible.

They were angry with Bramlet, who had hired them earlier that year to place bombs in front of two restaurants that refused to unionize. When the bombs failed to detonate, Bramlet refused to pay them. The Hanleys did not like getting stiffed, so they gladly accepted the contract on Bramlet. With a witness and a strong case, it did not take prosecutors long to convict the Hanleys. Tom Hanley died before ever seeing the inside of a prison cell. Gramby Hanley remains incarcerated.

Who Put the Hit on Barbara McNair's Husband?

Rick Manzie was a loser. A heroin addict with ties to the mob, Manzie's one success was probably his marriage to the beautiful African American singer and actress Barbara McNair. In a time when people of color struggled for an even break, Barbara McNair built a substantial career for herself in music, the movies, and on Broadway. In 1969, she was featured in Elvis Presley's last film, *Change of Habit.* That same year, she became the first African American woman to star in her own television series with her syndicated show running from 1969 to 1972. The musical variety show featured such guests as Wilson Pickett, Carlos Montoya, Della Reese, and Mahalia Jackson.

On July 22, 1972, with the TV show behind her and at the height of her career, Barbara McNair married her second husband, Rick Manzie, who was also her manager. The couple celebrated their nuptials at the Stardust with several friends. Las Vegas was their home now, and they would be living in McNair's twenty-room mansion on Bruce Street near the Sahara Hotel. Three months into the marriage, McNair was touched by scandal when she was arrested by federal agents at a Playboy Club in New Jersey. Unbeknown to her, she had signed for a package containing heroin at her Las Vegas home. She denied any knowledge of the drugs and posted the $10,000 bond. She was off the hook, but Manzie was indicted for the drugs. Through the work of a clever attorney, the charges were later dropped. Nonetheless, the publicity dinged McNair's career.

On December 15, 1976, Rick Manzie was at home alone in Las Vegas. His brother-in-law had left the mansion early that morning to do some grocery shopping. Barbara McNair was performing at a nightclub in Chicago and his mother had joined her there. Someone Manzie knew came to the door of the mansion and he let this person in. Whomever this person was, he shot and killed Manzie. The murder had all the earmarks of being a hit, but who was responsible and for what reason?

Police would later say there were no signs of forced entry, so suspicion fell on friends and acquaintances. Tony Spilotro, who himself would end up on the wrong end of a mob hit, was a good friend of Manzie, and he made it known that he wanted the killer of his friend found and dealt with. However, in his book *Rise and Fall of a Casino Mobster*, Frank Cullotta tells a very different story. He claims that Spilotro was responsible for the murder because Manzie was abusive to McNair, who Spilotro was having an affair with. Yet there is a third story; this one has Manzie being killed by the mob because he was planning a hit on an attorney. Regardless of where the truth of the Manzie murder lies, the killer (or killers) has never been brought to justice, but that is typical in mob hits.

Geri

She fell in love while still in Van Nuys High School. Shortly after graduating, she discovered she was pregnant, but Geri wanted more than just a job and a baby; she wanted a career—not just any career but one based on her natural good looks. She tried some swimsuit modeling and entered beauty contests, and she started winning prize money. However, her boyfriend decided she needed to be in Las Vegas in order to get that one big break. She agreed, and leaving him behind, she relocated to Las Vegas in the early 1960s with her mother and her daughter. Once settled, she dropped her Los Angeles boyfriend. Now she was truly on her own.

Getting a job was easy as she was stunning. Blonde and statuesque, Geri started running cocktails at the Tropicana, and every male eye in the place was on her. She relished the attention, knowing it meant more tokes, which boosted her pittance salary to a level that meant a comfortable lifestyle for herself, her daughter, and her mother. That is all Geri McGee really wanted. Aside from cocktails, she also worked as a topless dancer and a prostitute. It was a way to pay the bills until something better came along.

Geri's luck changed the night her escort, Tony Spilotro, introduced her to his longtime pal, Frank "Lefty" Rosenthal. Rosenthal was enchanted. Geri knew opportunity when it knocked. With Rosenthal, she had hit the bigtime. He had mob connections and he was secretly overseeing the mob's interest in four casinos: the Stardust, the Marina, the Hacienda, and the Fremont. He was a sports bettor and handicapper who had secured his spot when he developed the first sportsbook ever in a casino at the Stardust and brought sports gambling into Nevada casinos.

He was a powerful man in Las Vegas, and he made no secret of his interest in Geri. If she played her cards right, she would never have another money worry, ever. She did. He sent her a 2-carat diamond ring after their second date—as if she needed much convincing. They were married on May 4, 1969. However, this was not a happily ever after scenario. Frank Rosenthal did not know that his beautiful bride would continue her affair with Tony Spilotro, but she did. It is generally believed that the adulterous affair with his friend's wife is what ultimately led to the hit on Spilotro and his brother.

Certainly Geri's relationship with Spilotro did not help the marital problems the Rosenthals were having. Geri was not the wife to cook and sew and sit by the hearth awaiting her beloved husband's return. She liked to be where the action was. She was bored of staying home and missing out on Vegas's fast-paced nightlife. To fill the void, she shopped and lunched with the wives of Rosenthal's friends, including Mrs. Tony Spilotro, whom she was becoming very close with. However, domesticity was not Geri's strong suit.

After two children, she and Rosenthal were falling further apart. When she went out, Geri started staying out later and later. Eventually, she did not bother to come home at all; she was too busy drinking and doing drugs. When Tony Spilotro made the permanent move to Las Vegas in

1971, the affair intensified. However, he was not the only man she was seeing. They were in love, but theirs was a strange marriage. Tired of waiting for Geri, Lefty Rosenthal began dating other people as well. Just when the Rosenthals agreed to call it quits, one of them would have a change of heart and they would kiss and make up.

Seven years into their marriage, the bottom fell out of their financially stable world. Las Vegas authorities discovered that Lefty was running four casinos without the required Nevada gaming license. With his clout, Rosenthal thought it would be easy enough to get his license. He was wrong. The Nevada Gaming Control Board held a hearing on January 14, 1976, in which every member of the board voted to deny him a license.

> The applicant is a person whose licensing by the State would reflect or tend to reflect discredit upon the State of Nevada by reason of: A) A North Carolina court finding of guilt for conspiracy to bribe an amateur athlete; B) Testimony of Mickey Bruce in Senate subcommittee hearings that applicant attempted to bribe him to throw outcome of 1960 Oregon-Michigan football game; C) Statements by police officers Dardis and Clode to Senate subcommittee and to Florida Racing Commission that applicant admitted he was corrupting public officials in return for protection; D) The applicant's being barred from race tracks and pari-mutual operations in the State of Florida.

It was a bitter defeat for Rosenthal. He fought the decision with everything he had and lost. Life at home was no better. The Rosenthals' marriage was at a point that neither of them cared to try and save it. The tumultuous arguments were happening more often. By this time, Geri was a full-blown alcoholic and drug addict and Lefty was physically abusing her; at one time, she claimed that he had cracked her ribs and given her black eyes.

Both were still engaged in extramarital affairs. In 1981, after twelve years of marriage, they realized it was over. Both wanted out. As much as she loved them, she was unable to care for her children as she was a drunk. In the divorce, Rosenthal sued for, and was granted, custody of their two children; Geri fled to Los Angeles.

On Tuesday, November 6, 1982, when sunrise was still a few hours away, no one in the lobby of the Beverly Sunset Hotel noticed the bedraggled woman who stumbled in, strung out in a drug-induced stupor. Her legs were bruised; her blonde hair had not seen a hairbrush in a long time. She had the look of a loser. When someone finally noticed her, it was obvious the woman needed immediate medical attention.

An ambulance was called. Every eye watched as she was placed into the emergency vehicle and whisked away. Geraldine (Geri) McGee

Rosenthal died three days later on November 9, 1982. She was forty-six years old.

However, it was not over. Her body was barely cold when the rumors started. Her sister believed Geri had been murdered because she knew too much. Whatever Lefty Rosenthal believed, he kept to himself. The official cause of death was accidental overdose. Apparently, Lefty was not satisfied—either that or he did not want rumors of his having been responsible swirling around him for the rest of his life. Before she could be interred in her final resting place at Mount Sinai Memorial Cemetery in the Hollywood Hills, Geri's body would be subject to another autopsy—a $50,000 private autopsy that concluded with the same findings as the previous one had: Geri Rosenthal died of a whiskey, valium, and cocaine overdose.

Allen Glick, Marty Buccieri, and Tamara Rand

Tamara Rand was blonde, attractive, and very wealthy. She and Allen Glick were friends, although she was twenty years older than he was. They traveled in the same circles. Both were San Diegans. Rand was a real estate investor and Glick was an attorney. Both very much wanted a way in to Las Vegas gaming. Glick found his with an assist from the mob; he would be the mob's front man. Rand thought she had found hers when she loaned Glick $500,000 to help fund the purchase of Recrion Corp that owned the Stardust and the Fremont. Rand's half-million seemed paltry in comparison to the hefty $62.5 million loan from the Teamsters Pension Fund that was awarded to Glick.

That aside, Rand signed a contract as consultant with a yearly income of $100,000, even though she knew nothing about the operation of a casino. Rand believed her loan gave her 5 percent of Argent Corporation that owned the Hacienda. In the meantime, Marty Buccieri, a Caesars Palace casino pit boss who happened to be related to Chicago underboss Fiori "Fifi" Buccieri, hit Glick up for a $30,000 finder's fee. Marty Buccieri claimed to have influenced the approval of the multi-million-dollar Teamsters loan. In order to prove his point, Buccieri roughed up Glick.

However, Glick was steadfast; he would not pay. On May 13, 1975, three Caesars Palace patrons noticed a man slumped over the steering wheel of his car, obviously dead. The man had been shot in the back of the head; the car was a bloody mess. Marty Buccieri was through tossing cards and making demands. Although investigators believed Tony Spilotro was the killer, there was not enough evidence to bring a charge against Spilotro. The murder remains unsolved.

No sooner had Buccieri been relegated to past tense, than Glick and Tamara Rand got into a bitter argument. He finally told her the truth; she did not own a percentage of Argent Corporation and never would. She insisted that he had promised her that 5 percent and now he was saying that all she was supposed to get was the yearly $100,000 consultant fee. Things got dicey and Rand made a fatal mistake. She threatened to sue Glick for fraud and breach of contract. This, she assured him, would make all his dealings public, and there would be some explaining to do. Such threats do not go over well with the transparency-hating mob.

A few days after her argument with Glick, Tamara Rand was safe in her Mission Hills home when murder came calling. On November 9, 1975, she was busy making tea in her kitchen when her killer snuck in and shot her in the head five times; that ended her suit and Glick's debt. Again, Spilotro was the suspect of choice. The hit had been mob style—behind the ear and under the chin—but did Tony Spilotro do the killing? Investigators said her murder was similar to that of Sam Giancana, Marty Buccieri, and two other mob figures.

In 1978, FBI agents raided Glick's office at the Stardust and lowered the boom on the mob's cover operation. Glick was forced to sell out when Nevada took his gaming license. In 1982, Glick spoke to Federal Organized Crime Strike Force in Kansas City. Clearly, he saw himself as a victim. He would become a key witness against the mob and live to tell about it.

In 1985, Glick testified that the mob (via Lefty Rosenthal) demanded $10 million cash. When he told Rosenthal that he could not come up with that kind of money, he became angry. Glick insisted he had never been a front man and that he never realized he was involved with the mob until it was too late. According to his testimony, the mob had forced their way into his corporation through death threats and intimidation.

Bomb for Lefty Rosenthal

Frank "Lefty" Rosenthal was a creature of habit. Almost a month to the day before his ex-wife Geri wandered into the lobby of the Beverly Sunset Hotel dying of a drug and alcohol overdose, on October 4, 1982, Rosenthal was eating with three friends at the Tony Roma's on East Sahara. A devoted dad, Rosenthal grabbed two boxes of take-out food meant for his children, walked out into the balmy evening, crossed the parking lot, slid into the driver's seat, and started his yellow Caddy. Witnesses said the resulting explosion sounded like a freight train and blew the back windows out of the restaurant.

A car bombing generally sends its victim into the next world piece by piece, but not Lefty; that was his lucky day. General Motors had added a metal plate under the driver's seat on all Cadillac Eldorados to correct a balancing problem; it was this modification that had saved Lefty from being blown to bits. Rosenthal had also left the driver's door open while starting the car. This allowed him to jump from the car just before the gas tank caught fire. He was taken to the hospital and released a short time later. All he had sustained were a few minor scratches and bruises. Surely, he asked himself the question—what if his children had been in the backseat of that car with him? Just as surely, he knew the answer to that question only too well.

During his time in Las Vegas, Lefty had striven to be known as simply a businessman and a sports handicapper with his own weekly TV show. At least that was what he hoped the public believed. However, mob affiliate Lefty was more, much more, and he was wise enough to take the hint.

The bomb was a not-so-subtle threat to pack up, sell out, and leave Las Vegas behind; he did just that, fleeing first to California and later to Florida where he died of natural causes twenty-six years later on October 13, 2008. After his death, it was revealed that Lefty Rosenthal had been a top-echelon informant for the FBI. It was also revealed that his ex-wife Geri, though not a top-echelon informant, had also helped the FBI.

Tony Slept Here

Recently, mobster Tony Spilotro's old digs in Las Vegas went up for sale. An ordinary house in an ordinary neighborhood, the 2,400-sq. foot house located at 4675 Balfour Drive was offered at $420,000. Like most houses in Las Vegas, there is a rather large pool in the backyard. The thing is, Tony Spilotro lived, ate, slept, and made plans here. Those plans included the one-way trip he and his brother unwittingly took to that cornfield in Indiana. Yet there is no denying that the Las Vegas real estate market is hot. The Spilotro house sold fast; it did not even stay on the market a month. Tony would be pleased.

Anthony (the Ant) Spilotro arrived in a Las Vegas vastly different than that of Bugsy Siegel's time. It was 1971 and the mob, while still entrenched in Las Vegas, was losing its stranglehold on Nevada's gambling industry. By the late 1980s, it would be a done deal, both for the mob and for Spilotro.

Where Siegel was handsome and debonair, Spilotro was anything but. The Las Vegas of the 1970s was very different from the Las Vegas of Siegel's time. Using his wife's maiden name of Stuart, Spilotro ran the gift shop at Circus Circus. He was told to keep a low profile; the mob did not want undue attention. Instead of a garish or upscale mansion, the Spilotros moved into their middle-class digs on Balfour. Yet he could not (or would not) shy away from publicity. Tony loved publicity, power, and money, and we know how that worked out for him.

Philip Cline Hilton Fire

The MGM Grand Hotel fire early on the morning of November 21, 1980, was the worst disaster in Nevada's history, and one of the worst hotel fires in the world. Built in 1973, the MGM Grand Hotel Casino was ultra-modern and towered over many of the other hotels in the city; the twenty-six-story hotel at 3645 Las Vegas Blvd. ushered in a new and glamorous era in Las Vegas.

It was six days before Thanksgiving and the city was swarming with tourists; early in the morning, faulty wiring ignited a fire in the wall of the ground-floor deli. Employees tried to contain the fire, but it was already too late. The fast-moving flames fanned out and spread through the casino floor. Plastic molding, carpeting, wallpaper, and other such materials used in the hotel's construction quickly ignited and melted in the fire's wake, releasing toxic fumes into the air. There was no time to think and no time to run. People working and gambling in the ground-floor casino were overcome by the fumes and perished where they stood.

Of the over 5,000 people in the MGM Grand Hotel on the morning of November 21, 1980, 650 of them were injured enough to seek medical attention. Eighty-seven lost their lives in the fire. After lengthy investigations were completed, the charred rubble was cleared away. Even as rebuilding began, lawsuits totaling more than $200 million were filed. The ensuing investigation found that the MGM Grand fire might have been prevented had the entire building been fitted with sprinklers. The state of Nevada and Clark County acted quickly to enact some of the most stringent fire prevention building code laws in the United States.

Three months after the MGM Grand fire, the Las Vegas Hilton Casino Hotel was being retrofitted with an eye toward fire safety. The Las Vegas Hilton opened in July 1969 as the International, the largest hotel in the world, which had cost a hefty $60 million to build. The International was the city's first megaresort and would set a new Las Vegas standard with thirty floors, 1,500 rooms, and a casino floor space of 30,000 sq. feet. Barbara Streisand performed for sold-out crowds in the showroom. Staging a comeback, Elvis Presley was the next singer to entertain at the International. He did not disappoint; each of his fifty-eight consecutive performances sold out.

In 1970, the International was sold and renamed the Las Vegas Hilton. Elvis would continue appearing at the Las Vegas Hilton until 1976. Also, Muhammad Ali would lose his heavyweight championship to Leon Spinks at the Hilton in 1978.

It was Saturday, February 11, 1981, almost three years to the day of the Ali–Spinks championship fight. Phillip Bruce Cline, a newly hired room service busboy, was smoking marijuana when he started a fire in an eighth-floor lounge area. Cline would later insist that the fire had been started by accident when a curtain caught fire. In order to avert any suspicion, he raced down to the third floor and started another fire. As flames leapt up the sides of the building, Cline raced from room to room warning hotel guests to stay in their rooms. One of those who stayed in her penthouse room awaiting rescue that night was singer Natalie Cole, daughter of the late Nat King Cole. Later, in her memoir *Angel on my Shoulder*, Natalie Cole would refer to this time as rock bottom, claiming she had stayed in her suite on the twenty-sixth floor because she was smoking crack cocaine.

The MGM fire was on everyone's mind as firetrucks rolled up. Firefighters averted tragedy by using the techniques they had learned in the disastrous MGM Grand fire. When the blaze was contained, eight people were dead and 200 others were injured.

Phillip Bruce Cline attempted to play the hero, but investigators were suspicious of him when he wrote in his statement that he had filled a trashcan with fire. During a polygraph test, he confessed to starting the fire but insisted it had all been an accident. The curtains had caught on fire. Investigators tested the curtains and found that Cline was a liar as the drapes would not burn.

Cline was charged with eight counts of murder and one count of arson. Convicted of all the charges, Cline was sentenced to eight consecutive life terms without the possibility of parole, plus fifteen years for arson. The Hilton was closed for two weeks while damages to the building were assessed and necessary repairs made.

Courthouse Shooting

We generally assume that those who take a gun into a crowded location and try to kill as many people as possible are young men, but this is not always the case. Johnny Lee Wicks was sixty-six years old and retired, but he was not going to sit quietly and watch the world go by. Wicks had an enormous chip on his shoulder. He was convinced that the U.S. government was not treating him right, and his anger seethed. He was tired of seeing his Social Security benefits shrink. He had worked hard all his life, and now, because he had moved from California to Nevada, he was receiving over $300 dollars less than he had gotten in California. He filed a complaint against the Social Security Administration, claiming the reduction was because he was an African American.

"It's all about race. I am not a fool." Wicks had written in his complaint. In September 2009, a judge tossed the case when Wicks did not follow the appeals process. This may have helped to push Johnny Lee Wicks over the edge.

On January 4, 2010, early Monday morning before sunrise, he set fire to his condo. He would not be coming back. Monday is the beginning of a new work week for Las Vegas nine–five office workers. Those who worked in the building and jurors, fulfilling their civic duty, started filing into the Loyd D. George Federal District Courthouse on S. Las Vegas Blvd around 8 a.m.

Johnny Lee Wicks had made his decision. Armed with a Mossberg 500 shotgun, he entered the lobby of the courthouse. Nine floors up, former U.S. Senators Harry Reid and John Ensign kept offices. Luckily neither senator was anywhere near the shooting when Wicks opened fire at the security check-in. A security officer who was several years older than Wicks was struck in the chest and killed. A deputy marshal sustained injuries but survived. With federal marshals returning fire, Wicks ran from the building. He did not get far. Marshals followed, firing; a bullet hit him in the head, killing him instantly.

After the shooting, Senator Reid tweeted the following: "This tragedy in Las Vegas serves as a reminder of the sacrifices all law enforcement officials make on our behalf each and every day."

David Strickland Suicide

On Friday night, November 20, 1998, three-time world poker champion Stu Unger checked into the rundown, third-rate Oasis Hotel on 1731 S. Las Vegas Blvd. For a man who had won and lost millions, it was a strange choice as the hotel is one of those places where you can rent a room by the hour. It is not in the classiest area of town and certainly does not offer the poshest of digs. Nonetheless, Unger paid $120 for two nights and was given the key to room fourteen. It was the last time anyone would ever see him alive.

Unger's body was discovered on Sunday night, lying face up in his hotel bed; Clark County coroner Ron Flud's official cause of death was accidental death. The forty-five-year-old had succumbed to coronary atherosclerosis. Although Unger was an admitted drug user, there was no drug paraphernalia found in the room.

On Monday, March 22, 1999, David Strickland failed to appear as scheduled in a Los Angeles court. In December, the actor had pleaded no contest to a charge of cocaine possession and was ordered into rehabilitation and placed on probation; on this day, he was slated to attest to his progress. Concerned over Strickland's no show, his friend, Brooke Shields, hired a private detective to locate him.

The twenty-nine-year-old actor seemed to have everything to live for. He was a regular in the popular television series *Suddenly Susan*; also, the movie *Force of Nature* in which he had co-starred with Sandra Bullock and Ben Affleck was just hitting the box office. However, it was not enough.

On Monday afternoon, a maid discovered Strickland's body in room twenty-one at the Oasis Hotel. After a wild binge weekend of drugs and booze, he had torn a sheet into strips, fashioned a noose, wrapped it tightly around his neck, and hanged himself from a beam in his room.

Suicide by Plane

Contractor John Covarrubias was well-liked by his employees. To them, he was an honest, fair, and friendly man—a good boss. He may have been all these things, but there was more to John Covarrubias than his employees realized. He was a miserably unhappy man. He and his ex-wife Nellie had been divorced for six months, and he could not cope with the single life. He desperately wanted his wife back. Around 11 p.m. on April 10, 1965, he went to her crowded bar the Branding Iron Bar in nearby Pittman (Henderson) to talk her into getting back together with him.

This time, he hoped, she would agree to come back to him. His hopes were dashed when she refused his overtures, telling him that no matter what he did or said, they were finished. He was enraged. "You don't have long to live." Covarrubias screamed at her. "I'll fly my plane into this bar and kill you!" He turned to two men who were sitting at the bar. "She doesn't have long to live," he said.

They had heard marital arguments before and did not take the threat seriously; Neither did Nellie, but she should have. It was Saturday night. The bar was busy. She turned from him to see to customers with empty glasses at the end of the bar. When she walked away from him, John Covarrubias angrily stormed out of the bar. He meant to see his threat through.

A light rain was falling as the bright green Cessna 210 twin-engine taxied down the runway at Las Vegas McCarran Field. Covarrubias piloted his plane across the Phoenix Highway (Boulder Highway) flying low. A witness estimated the plane was only about 3 feet from the ground when it flew toward the bar and smashed into the parking lot. Witnesses described it as "a Kamikaze sort of thing."

"He was aiming for the bar." Clark County Sheriff's Lieutenant Bill Witte told newspaper reporters. "The only thing that stopped him were the cars."

The crash left a 30-foot hole in the building. People ran screaming from the bar. Many of them were injured by the falling debris. One was severely burned in the plane's gasoline explosion. The only death was that of John Covarrubias; he was thrown from the cockpit onto the top of a burning car. A year after the incident, Nellie Covarrubias was sued in District Court by twelve people who claimed their automobiles were damaged in the crash.

Three years later, on August 2, 1968, another man facing divorce decided to end his life in a similar manner. With no waiting period, marriage and divorce can happen fast in Las Vegas. The Shaws had been married three weeks when Mrs. Shaw filed for divorce. This depressed her husband, Everett Wayne Shaw, who thought the marriage would last forever. The airplane mechanic stole a Cessna 180 from the airfield in Jean and flew toward Las Vegas. He was set to end it all at the new Landmark tower, which was 297 feet tall (making it the tallest building in Nevada at that time).

Apparently, Shaw changed his mind at the last minute and pulled up; however, it was too late—the plane clipped the top of the Landmark tower and crashed into the Las Vegas Convention Center on the other side of the street.

Like Covarrubias's *kamikaze* suicide, Everett Wayne Shaw was the only person to die in the plane crash. For those who may have wondered why, he had thoughtfully left suicide notes in both his apartment and that of his ex-wife.

Alex Egyed

In a town of winners and losers, Alex Egyed was a winner. He lived an enviable lifestyle that most people only dream about. While others in this town might worry how they will pay their bills, Egyed had no such money worries. He was not a penny-pinching loser trying to break even; Egyed's knowledge of computer technology had paid off in a big way. He was also a millionaire many times over. His wife, Virginia, was the former wife of Stanley Mallin, who was co-owner of Caesars Palace and Circus Circus. Alex, Virginia, and her teenage daughter from her previous marriage to Mallin lived in a luxurious home in the exclusive enclave Rancho

Circle on the right side of town. Rancho Circle was one of Las Vegas's first masterplan communities, a place that boasted neighbors with deep pockets, neighbors like singer Phyllis McGuire, former main squeeze of long-dead mobster Sam Giancana.

Like all couples the Egyeds occasionally fought, and when they fought, Alex got depressed and worried about losing Virginia. What if she had another man? What if she should leave him? The thought made him crazy. He could not face life without Virginia.

One night in September 1984, Virginia's teenage daughter had a friend (Sandy Shaw) sleeping over. The Egyeds were at a charity event when they got into a heated argument. Virginia was so angry she refused to ride home with Alex and left in a separate vehicle. She was going to the home they shared to pick up her daughter, then to another friend's home. Later that evening, she was gathering a few items with her friends, Levy and Betty Di Fiore, at the Egyed mansion when Alex arrived, still upset. Ignoring the Di Fiores, Alex pulled Virginia aside, demanding that she talk with him. She brushed him off as this was not the time—there were guests in the house. Guests or not, Egyed wanted to talk. He tried once more to get her to discuss their argument. She brushed him off once more.

He furiously raced through the house and retrieved his hidden gun. It was loaded and he was ready to make sure that Virginia would listen— and she would talk. Then he changed his mind. He would not give her the opportunity to do so.

Egyed walked into his step-daughter's room where he found the two teenagers and Betty Di Fiore. Di Fiore opened her mouth to speak. He shot her in the head, then walked downstairs to the kitchen where he found Virginia. Without a word, he pointed the gun at her and fired. Then he walked out to the car in the driveway, where Levy Di Fiore and a friend were hiding. Egyed shot Di Fiore in the head, turned, and went back into the mansion. Three people were dead, but he was not finished. Egyed put the gun to his head and he pulled the trigger.

Sandy Shaw—The Show and Tell Murder

According to the odds makers, the odds of winning a million-dollar megabucks jackpot is 1 in 50 million. Now, what are the odds that a person would witness a murder three times in the span of two years? Staggering, no doubt, and yet Sandy Shaw did just that. She was only thirteen years old when she witnessed the murder–suicide of her friend's mother and step-father (Virginia and Alex Egyed). Not long afterward, she was walking home from school when she witnessed a man run up behind his wife. Before the startled woman could run, he shot and killed her.

Two years later, she was fifteen and being pursued by twenty-one-year-old James "Cotton" Thiede-Kelly, a fugitive Canadian drug dealer. Cotton liked the blonde cheerleader's looks and he moved quickly. After their initial meeting at Circus Circus arcade, he claimed to want to take nude photos of her. She might have been only fifteen, but she was not naïve. Sandy Shaw knew that taking nude photos of her was not all Cotton wanted from her.

She turned him down, but Cotton was persistent. He continued to call her house at all hours of the day and night. In desperation, she asked her longtime friend eighteen-year-old Troy Kell to rough Cotton up and make him stop hounding her. Kell enlisted his friend Billy Merritt to help make Cotton see reason. A plan was made.

For her part, all Sandy had to do was to lure Cotton into the desert where they would show James Cotton Thiede-Kelly that Sandy meant business and to leave her alone. The task was easy for Sandy. Cotton was so smitten with her that he believed she was sincere when she agreed to go on a date with him on the night of September 29, 1986.

As Cotton and Sandy drove along the lonely desert highway, they came upon a pair of hitchhikers. Sandy insisted he stop and give them a lift. Eager to please, he went against his better judgment and stopped for the hitchhikers. He had no idea that the two young men were actually Troy Kell and Billy Merritt, friends of Sandy's.

The car was barely back on the highway when Sandy said, "I have to pee." Eager to please again, Cotton pulled up alongside the roadway and stopped the car. Sandy jumped out and stumbled into the desert where she pretended to trip. Still playing the "Knight in Shining Armor" role, Cotton ran after her to check on her safety. This was their cue. Kell and Merritt jumped out of the car. Before he realized what was happening, Cotton was overtaken and shot six times in the face by Troy Kell.

Sandy, Kell, and Merritt helped themselves to what money Cotton had in his wallet and left the body where it lay. If not for teenage bravado and boastfulness, it might have been years before the mystery surrounding the whereabouts of James Cotton Thiede-Kelly was solved. However, Sandy wanted to show off. She led some of her friends from Rancho High School out to see the dead man who had bothered her. Even if she did not say it, the message was implied—do not mess with Sandy Shaw. This was well before social media; there would be no selfies with a dead man. However, teenagers being what they are, they talked and word got around fast.

A dead man in the desert was impressive, especially when it was one of their peers that was responsible for his being there. Soon groups of teens were making their way out to the desert to see the rotting Cotton, hence the reason the murder would later be dubbed "the Show and Tell Murder."

As Cotton moldered, one of the teenagers was struck by conscience. She told her parents about the cadaver, pointing the finger at Sandy, Troy, and Billy. The three teens were arrested and charged with murder. Troy Kell tried to protect Sandy by denying she had anything to do with the murder. He was the sole killer, he stated, not Sandy. Merritt agreed. His attempt at saving Sandy did little good. Both Sandy and Troy Kell were convicted and sentenced to life without parole. Merritt served twelve years, but after a number of violent crimes, he was back in prison. serving life without parole as well.

After serving twenty-one years, Sandy Shaw was paroled from prison, free to start a new life in Las Vegas. Troy Kell's life took a different path. In an inmate exchange program, he was sent to prison in Gunnison, Utah. There he tapped into his white supremacist roots. After being involved in several race-related fights, he stabbed an African American inmate sixty-seven times on July 6, 1994. Sixteen years later, love-struck Troy Kell. On December 9, 2010, Kell married his fiancée, whose name was not made public. How the marriage has fared is anybody's guess. At time of writing, Troy Kell is awaiting his execution by firing squad.

The Death of Rose Azbill

Ed and Rose Mapel had been married over forty years when he died, leaving her a very wealthy widow. With all her money, it did not take the lonely sixty-one-year-old widow long to find a new husband. The groom was Sylvester Azbill, twenty years her junior. They married on September 20, 1967. Rose was infatuated and could not have made a worse choice. Azbill, who had unsuccessfully ran as a Democrat for the office of Nevada secretary of state, was in love when they married but not with his wife. Azbill's love was deep, but it was only for his wife's money.

Three months after the vows, the marriage was over. On December 27, 1967, Rose realized that Sylvester had only married her for her money and she was angry. After telling Sylvester that she planned on divorcing him, the two of them did what they often did. They started drinking and arguing in the master bedroom. Sylvester had had a taste of wealth and he had no intentions of losing his grip on his wife's money; a divorce would surely do just that. He raised his crutch and struck her as she lay in bed. When he was sure that she was incapacitated, Azbill doused the helpless woman with lighter fluid and struck a match.

In the guest house, Azbill's teenage son and friends saw smoke pouring from the main house. The teenagers raced to the main house where Azbill met them, saying the oven was burning. The boys found nothing wrong with the oven and ran outside where they broke the bedroom window and found Rose Mapel burned to death in her bed.

The teenagers would remember a lot about that day and the strange behavior of Sylvester Azbill.

They testified against Azbill, who was convicted and sentenced to life without the possibility of parole. He would appeal and try for parole several times over the years, all without success. Sylvester Azbill died in prison several years ago.

New in Town

People come to Las Vegas for any number of reasons—some are running from something; some are looking for something. On April 22, 1989, Eleanor (Ellie) Panzarella arrived in Las Vegas. One of the first people she met was a man by the name of Ruben Varela, who was also new in town. He seemed like a decent person to Ellie, so she agreed to let him keep some of his stuff at her apartment she had just rented on E. Harmon. While he moved his things into the apartment, neighbors Rose and D'Agostino dropped by to introduce themselves. Ellie complained about not having any dishes or glasses, and Rose offered to give her some. When Frank D'Agostino came to the apartment bearing the gifts, he offered to buy cocaine for Ruben and Ellie. It sounded like a good deal, so Ruben gave him $200 to get them some for later.

That night, Ellie and Ruben went out on the town, drinking and gambling. The more they drank, the more Ellie realized that Ruben might not be as nice as she first assumed. This was especially true after they got into a heated argument. He shoved her. She shoved back. Then, Ruben Varela angrily stormed off, leaving her alone in the casino. However, Ellie made friends fast. Before the night was over, she had a new friend in Jack Green.

During their time together, she admitted to being frightened in case Ruben returned to her apartment and tried to start another fight with her. Jack Green offered to go to the apartment with her to make sure that did not happen, and it did not.

However, Ruben Varela was angry at Ellie and Frank D'Agostino. He caused a disturbance in the apartment complex and got into a screaming match with D'Agostino, who still had not given him the cocaine he had paid for. When he finally got tired, Ruben left the complex, and seeing the

La Concha motel lobby. (*Library of Congress*)

Bingo game, *c.* 1950s. (*Library of Congress*)

Left: Roulette, *c.* 1950s.
(*Library of Congress*)

Below: Thunderbird.
(*Author's collection*)

Golden nugget. (*Author's collection*)

Spring Mountain Ranch—site of the Krupp diamond robbery. (*Photo by Bill Oberding*)

Close-up of Spring Mountain Ranch house site of Krupp Diamond Robbery. (*Photo by Bill Oberding*)

Spring Mountain Ranch house site of Krupp Diamond robbery. (*Photo by Bill Oberding*)

Above: Wayne Newton photographs (*Carol M. Highsmith Archive, Library of Congress, Prints and Photographs Division*)

Right: Painting of Rosalie Maxwell. (*Courtesy of Frank LaPena*)

Frank LaPena. (*Photo courtesy Frank LaPena*)

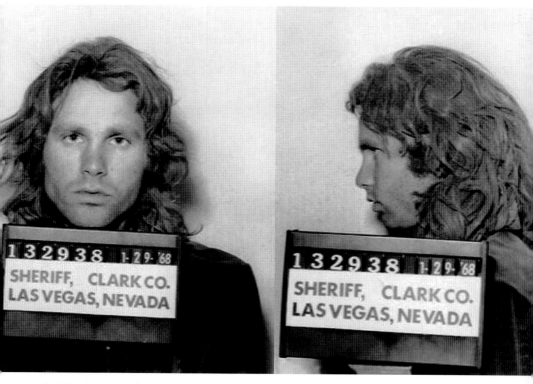

Jim Morrison's mugshot.

Luxor aerial view. (*Carol M. Highsmith Archive, Library of Congress, Prints and Photographs Division*)

Mandalay Bay. (*Carol M. Highsmith Archive, Library of Congress, Prints and Photographs Division*)

The high-roller. (*Photo by Bill Oberding*)

High-roller pods. (*Photo by Bill Oberding*)

Next pod up close. (*Photo by Bill Oberding*)

Las Vegas Strip at night. (*Carol M. Highsmith Archive, Library of Congress, Prints and Photographs Division*)

El Rancho Hotel, *c.* 1940s. (Author's collection)

The Flamingo, *c.* 1940s and 1950s. (*Author's collection*)

Riviera billboard, *c.* 1960. (*Author's collection*)

Riviera, *c.* 1950s. (*Author's collection*)

Folies Bergere pamphlet.

Sands at night from an old postcard. (*Author's collection*)

The dunes. (*Author's collection*)

Styled in breath-taking splendor and elegance, America's most spectacular new 700-seat theatre-restaurant, brings the Continental Touch to Las Vegas! Here you will thrill to lavish productions featuring the stars of Hollywood, Broadway, Paris, the World! Here, too, you will delight in cuisine prepared by world-renowned chefs and served in the classic Continental tradition.

Stardust program mailer.

Showgirls, *c.* 1960s. (*Author's collection*)

Tropicana gaming. (*Carol M. Highsmith Archive, Library of Congress, Prints and Photographs Division*)

Frank "Lefty" Rosenthal. (*Special Collections, University Libraries, University Nevada, Las Vegas*)

Opposite above: The landmark. (*Author's collection*)

Opposite below: Las Vegas night high tower. (*Library of Congress*)

The million-dollar display from an old postcard.

Right: Bonnie Harper, center (author's mom); Roy Harper, right (author's dad); and Sylvia Ngar, right, with Binion's million-dollar display.

Below: Benny Binion's horseshoe. (*Library of Congress*)

Posse members pose with Queho remains. (*Special Collections, University Libraries, University Nevada, Las Vegas*)

At the entrance of Queho's Cave hideaway. (*Special Collections, University Libraries, University Nevada, Las Vegas*)

Mandalay Bay, where Stephen Paddock took aim and fired at his victims. (*Photo by Bill Oberding*)

Remembrance Wall in honor of victims of the mass shooting. (*Photo by Bill Oberding*)

Las Vegas sign in remembrance of the mass shooting victims of Stephen Paddock. (*Photo by Bill Oberding*)

Above: Rocks in the remembrance garden in honor of victims of the mass shooting. (*Photo by Bill Oberding*)

Right: The Kiel Brothers from postcard. (*Special Collections, University Libraries, University Nevada, Las Vegas*)

Stardust program/mailer.

The Bellagio. (*Photo by Bill Oberding*)

Bellagio photographs. (*Carol M. Highsmith Archive, Library of Congress, Prints and Photographs Division*)

New York, New York—site of Cameron James Kennedy's ill-fated robbery. (*Photo by Bill Oberding*)

Tony Spilotro and his attorney, Oscar Goodman. (*Special Collections, University Libraries, University Nevada, Las Vegas*)

The Desert Inn, *c.* early 1950s. (*Author's collection*)

Casino gaming, *c.* 1950s and 1960s. (Author's collection)

The courthouse and post office, later Mob Museum. (*Library of Congress*)

Post office courthouse, c. 1960. (*Library of Congress*)

Left: The Sands. (*Author's collection*)

Below: Ronald Reagan Las Vegas floorshow from an old postcard. (*Author's collection*)

all-clear, Jack Green did as well. Now Ellie was alone. Sometime during the night of the 23rd and the morning of the 24th, Frank D'Agostino visited her in her apartment; he went back and forth from his apartment to Ellie's. At one point, Rose saw him wrap a steak knife in baking soda and a newspaper. If she wondered what he why he was doing this, she did not ask.

It was well after midnight when Ellie's next-door neighbor woke to the sound of someone, or something, being banged against the wall. She was almost certain that she heard the sound of a woman's muffled cry for help. However, she did not have a telephone. The next morning, everything seemed okay, so she did not contact the police. In the D'Agostino apartment, it was a very different situation. Rose was barely out of bed when Frank returned to the apartment. He had blood on his face, clothes, and hands. He was sweating profusely. When he undressed to take a shower, his penis and thighs were streaked in blood.

Frightened, Rose looked at the knife he had brought back with him. Chunks of flesh and a black curly hair were attached to it. Evidence would later show that Panzarella died of two stab wounds to the heart and had been stabbed over thirty times. "What did you do?" She asked.

In reply, he tossed a plastic bag on the sofa. She looked inside to find several $100 bills and a number of diamond rings, a necklace, and other pieces of jewelry. She knew. Try as she might, she could not run from the truth when she realized that he also had Ellie's driver's license and credit card in his possession. No one would readily give up those two items, but she was not the only person who knew what Frank had done.

A friend started staying with Frank and Rose shortly after the murder. He accompanied Frank D'Agostino to Ellie's apartment where he watched as Frank sprayed perfume in the air as a way to cover the smell of the decomposing body that lay on a bloodied mattress. When he questioned Frank, he told him that Ruben had murdered Ellie; it was a lie, and the friend knew it.

Over the next few days, they pawned the dead woman's jewelry for $490 and returned to her apartment. Trying to destroy evidence, Frank wrapped her body in a carpet and set it alight with rubbing alcohol. On May 2, employees of the apartment complex discovered Ellie's partially burned body. With the police swarming the area, D'Agostino and Rose packed up and headed to Phoenix. After a brief stay in which Rose gave birth to a child, they moved on to Tampa, Florida, and tried to forget all about Ellie Panzarella.

Ten months after the murder, D'Agostino and Rose got into a heated argument that escalated until he physically abused her. Fearing for her safety, she called the police. While she was telling them about the abuse, she also told police about the sordid story of Ellie Panzarella's murder. She had not reported the crime earlier because she was afraid of what Frank might do to her and her family. Frank D'Agostino was arrested, and while he cooled his heels in a Tampa jail, Rose was flown back to Las Vegas to give details in the unsolved murder.

She would be the state's principal witness against D'Agostino. Due to her cooperation, some charges against her were dropped and she received some secret witness payments. In 1990, Frank D'Agostino was found guilty of first-degree murder and sentenced to death for killing Ellie Panzarella. He appealed the death penalty and asked for a new trial at the Nevada Supreme Court in 1997. The court denied him a new trial, other than a penalty hearing in which the death penalty was vacated and D'Agostino was given two life sentences without the possibility of parole.

The Death of Karen Blackwell

Ten days after her murder, Karen Blackwell's body was discovered in the trunk of a car in 1986. The twenty-six-year-old prostitute had been stabbed forty-five times. Her killer, twenty-one-year-old John Espiredion Valerio, was convicted of the murder two years later and sentenced to death. With appeals, the death penalty drags on. So it was that at the age of fifty-two, Valerio saw a federal appeals court overturn his death sentence because he did not get a fair trial. The appeals court found that unconstitutional juror instructions may have led to Valerio receiving the death penalty in the first place.

However, you do not get to stab someone forty-five times and walk away a free man; Valerio did not. While he talked about being a changed man who had found religion, Valerio did not deny his heinous crime. The changed man avoided the death penalty, but he will spend the rest of his life behind bars with no chance of parole.

Craig Titus and Kelly Ryan

They were blessed with prizewinning genes. They were the beautiful people of bodybuilding. Wannabe champions on the edge of stardom, Craig Titus and Kelly Ryan knew how to pose their tanned, oiled, and athletic bodies. They also knew how to compete. Pumped up with steroids, Titus was a Mr. Olympian competitor and a former 1996 bodybuilding champion. Kelly had won her share of prizes as well. A crowd-pleaser, she was a former fitness international winner—never the top winner, but never the lowest on the rung either.

They were the envy of their weight-pumping buddies, but there was a dark side to Titus and Ryan. None of their bodybuilding buddies knew that when they were not in the gym pumping iron, Titus was using steroids, and together, they were using a lot of other drugs. He had a criminal record. She was the cute and talented girl next door. They were making a lot of money. Eventually, they might have made it all the way to the top, but they did not; their egos were just too big, bigger perhaps than Titus's bulging muscles.

Their lives started falling apart when Melissa James moved in with them. In the beginning, she was there in the home as their personal assistant, answering correspondence and seeing that their schedules were moving smoothly—grunt work, if you will. Yet Melissa James was young and talented in her own right, a dancer with the lithe body of one who's spent years at the ballet barre, perfecting her plies and her jettes. Craig noticed, and Kelly noticed that he was noticing. Even under Kelly's watchful eye, an affair ensued. Melissa James fell into the same drug trap that held Kelly Ryan and Craig Titus. She was hooked—perhaps she had even fallen deeper into drug addiction than either Ryan or Titus.

At least, that was the story they would be telling when what was left of Melissa James was discovered in a burning Jaguar out in the middle of nowhere in the desert. For whatever reason, they had decided to do away with the problem of the third wheel in their relationship; he cruelly beat and killed her, then stuffed her body in the trunk of Kelly's jaguar and set it on fire. This was not the smartest of moves, but then they were not on the covers of the fitness and muscle mags for their brains.

After telling numerous lies to Melissa James's mother, Ryan and Titus packed up personal items and a thick bankroll of cash and tried to run away. They were arrested on the other end of the country and extradited back to Nevada. The bodybuilding world was in shock. Meanwhile, Titus's and Ryan's stories kept changing.

At trial, Kelly Ryan denied killing Melissa James:

> I am truly truly sorry. I know I did not kill but aid once Melissa died. I was not in a state of mind emotionally or physically to make the right decisions or to, oh God, to take appropriate control of what was happening. I'm truly sorry. I ask for forgiveness.

Craig Titus pleaded guilty to second-degree murder, kidnapping, and arson. Kelly Ryan pleaded guilty to arson and no contest to arson and battery with a deadly weapon. The mother of Melissa James begged the judge for the maximum sentence.

In August 2008, Judge Jackie Glass was tough. She called Kelly Ryan's tears "crocodile tears" and Craig Titus "a murderer," and then sentenced Ryan to six to twenty-six years and Titus from twenty-one to fifty-one years. Divorced from Craig Titus, Kelly Ryan was released on parole in October 2017. Her ex-husband, Craig Titus, will not be eligible for parole until December 2026.

Benny Binion and the Murders of Bill Coulthard and Marvin Shumate

Benny Binion came to Las Vegas in 1946 with his family, a suitcase full of money, and a criminal record that might have kept a lesser person from ever obtaining a Nevada state gaming license—not so for Benny Binion. Five years after arriving in town, Binion bought the Apache Hotel and the Eldorado Club; he revamped them into Binion's Horseshoe Casino. Downtown Vegas, A.K.A. Glitter Gulch, would see some changes with Binion's casino. It was the first casino in Vegas to have carpeting and high-limit tables and to offer comps to gamblers who spent big and those who did not—a customer was a customer.

Texas had been trying to get the state of Nevada to extradite Binion from the moment he left the Lone Star State. However, Nevada would not budge. When the feds made a demand, Nevada could not ignore them. Benny Binion was charged with eight counts of tax evasion. Benny paid $500,000 in delinquent tax and pleaded guilty to four counts on December 7, 1953. Four of the eight counts were dropped, and Binion was sent to Leavenworth for four years. In order to pay his back taxes and keep the casino open, he sold the majority share to Joe W. Brown, a fellow gambler and oilman. Yet this was just until Benny returned from the pen.

While Brown held the majority interest in the Horseshoe, it was rebuilt and the famous "million-dollar" display added.

The display was made of 10,000 $100 bills stacked and surrounded by a horseshoe. The display allowed patrons to have their pictures taken with a million bucks (glass-enclosed, of course), and thousands of them did. It was a great tourism gimmick; Binion liked the idea and would keep it when he took back the reins of his Horseshoe. The Horseshoe would continue to revamp the million-dollar display over the years.

Benny Binion would come up for parole a year later. While he cooled his heels at Leavenworth, his friends in Las Vegas began a letter-writing campaign to help him at the parole board. Gus Greenbaum, Wilbur Clark, and former Las Vegas Mayor Ernie Cragin all wrote letters on Benny's behalf at the urging of Hank Greenspun, owner of *The Sun* newspaper. His friends were powerful, and their words carried enough weight that Benny was released.

When Benny got out of prison, he bought out Joe W. Brown's interest and continued operating the Horseshoe as a family endeavor. As they got older, Binion's sons supervised gaming while his wife, Teddy Jane, acted as book-keeper.

Binion is long dead. His beloved Horseshoe is no longer owned and operated by his family. There were too many financial woes. His son, Ted, died under mysterious circumstances in 1998; his death was a *cause célèbre*, the center of a murder trial that rocked Las Vegas. The media reported all the titillating details, and there were plenty—illegal drugs, a love triangle, the much younger live-in girlfriend that he met at a topless bar, and a buried crate full of silver coins. After convictions that got tossed out, another jury found that Ted died as a result of his own bad judgment. He was a heroin addict, done in by an accidental overdose.

Years before Ted shot up his last, he was seen as a quick way to wealth by taxi driver Marvin Shumate. All Shumate had to do was kidnap Ted and hold him until his dad, Benny Binion, coughed up the money to set the young man free. Small-time conman Shumate had his plan all worked out. Then, he did something stupid. He brought in a partner. Then Shumate changed his mind about the kidnapping logistics. Perhaps it would be best not to leave a witness. Killing young Binion seemed the best course of action, after all. The partner had not bargained on murder, especially that of Ted Binion. He wanted no part of Shumate or his plan, so he ran to Benny Binion and spilled Shumate's secrets.

No one crossed Benny Binion. He loved his family dearly. He did not take kindly to Shumate's plan. After work, Shumate stopped in for a drink at a neighborhood bar; it would be the last time anyone, other than his killer, saw him alive.

In December 1967, when next seen, Shumate was dead, shot to death near Sunrise Mountain. Robbery was not the motive. The dead man's money was still in his wallet. No one was ever charged for Shumate's murder, but as more details came out, it was unofficially believed that Binion ordered the hit. The message was loud and clear—do not mess with Benny Binion's family.

July 25, 1972, was a hot day in Vegas. The temperature was well over 100 degrees when Bill Coulthard slid into the driver's seat of his Cadillac on the third-floor parking garage of the Nevada Bank building where his law office was. He put his key in the ignition and turned it. He was killed instantly as the car exploded in a roar that decapitated Coulthard, severed his legs, and sent debris flying in all directions, shattering light fixtures on the first floor of the ten-story building. Nearby cars were demolished in the ensuing fire.

Coulthard's body was ripped apart and so badly burned that the only way a positive identification could be made was through the use of dental records. Investigators later determined that a clothespin wired to the ignition of Coulthard's caddy was the bomb's trigger. They estimated that anywhere from two to four sticks of dynamite had been placed under the engine near the steering column.

As a former FBI agent, Coulthard probably had his share of enemies, and as an attorney, he surely had a client who was not happy with the way his case was handled. Yet it was Benny Binion's name that was unofficially tossed around as the person behind the car bombing. Coulthard's and Binion's recent negotiations had been bitter. Coulthard owned much of the land Benny's Horseshoe sat upon. When it came time to renew the lease, Coulthard refused to do so and had negotiated the sale of the property with one of Benny's competitors. This left Benny in the lurch and with little choice. Miraculously after the bombing, Benny got a new 100-year lease on the property at low rent.

Like Benny Binion, William (Bill) Coulthard had been a Las Vegas old-timer. He first set foot in the city as a twenty-three-year-old in 1939. Sent by the FBI as the city's first resident agent, he would serve in this capacity until he left the FBI in 1945. It was during his time as an FBI agent that he met, fell in love with, and married Lena Silvagni, whose family owned various real estate holdings including the Apache Hotel. He opened his law practice in 1946 and would continue at it until his death in 1972. Coulthard briefly dabbled in politics and was elected as a Nevada assemblyman from 1951 to 1954.

At her death in 1955, Lena left her share of the family real estate holdings to Coulthard. Part of this real estate figured in the rancorous disagreement between Benny Binion and Bill Coulthard.

The Death of Willebaldo Dorantes Antonio

Willebaldo Dorantes Antonio and Caren Chali were young and in love, but they were taking their time. They had been losers in love before and were willing to gamble that their relationship would turn out better than those previous. Like all lovers, they dreamed of building a bright and happy future together.

As undocumented immigrants, they were used to taking chances. They minded their own business, kept their heads down, and worked at the Nathan's hotdog stand inside the Luxor. They were happy, except for one problem—Omar Rueda Denvers, Caren's former boyfriend who was also the father of her child. They had met in Guatemala and migrated to the United States together. Yet they had only been in the United States for fifteen days when he met a new woman and dumped Chali; her heart was broken, but she had moved on and now he wanted her back. However, Chali no longer cared what he wanted. She was happy and in love with Willebaldo. Omar was furious when she told him so.

At 4 a.m., on May 7, 2007, Caren and Willebaldo finished their eight-hour shift and walked hand-in-hand to his car in the Luxor parking garage. As they neared his 1995 Dodge, they noticed that someone had placed a Styrofoam coffee cup on the car's hood. "Get in the car." Willebaldo told her gently. Caren reach for the door handle idly watching as Willebaldo lifted the cup; suddenly, there was a deafening boom.

Later, Chali would testify for the prosecution in the case against Omar Rueda Denvers. Speaking through an interpreter, she said, "I turned around to where Willebaldo was … he wasn't there anymore. I ran around the car … I only remember that he didn't have his fingers."

The explosion shredded his hand, and a piece of metal struck him in the head, lodging in his brain and killing him instantly. Within four days of Willebaldo's death, the police would arrest Omar Rueda Denvers and Porfirio Duarte Herrera, the man who had made the bomb for him.

During opening statements, the prosecutor said of the bomb, "It was an extremely powerful bomb. It was by its design and how it was structured to detonate designed for one sole purpose and that was to kill."

In describing Willebaldo's injuries, Luxor security guard Scott Casey testified, "He was laying on his side. He had a pool of blood around his head. His right hand was gone. Skin was hanging off of his knuckles. He kind of moaned and shrugged." Both Denvers and Duarte-Herrera were found guilty of murder and sentenced to life in prison without the possibility of parole. Caren Chali and her child were deported. Some love stories just do not have happy endings.

Palomino Club

There is an old saying that lightning never strikes twice in the same place. This is not true when it comes to murder. The Palomino Club is a North Las Vegas landmark. It is also the only strip club in Vegas that offers alcohol and entertainment that includes nude dancers. There is a reason for this. The Palomino was opened in 1969 by Paul Perry and was thus grandfathered in before such restrictions were placed on strip clubs. Yet nothing lasts forever, and that license is soon set to expire. In 2000, Perry's son, Jack, was co-managing the club along with Kenneth Rowan. It was a good arrangement until the morning of December 27, 2000. That was when Jack Perry shot and killed Kenneth Rowan at the Palomino.

While Perry readily admitted to the killing, he would not give a reason. It was thought that an argument between the two men over Perry's belief that Rowan was trying to buy the club and shut him out was the impetus Ed Kane, Chief Deputy District Attorney Clark County was perplexed and admitted we may never know all the details of the murder. In court, Perry apologized to both families and claimed to be remorseful. He then made a deal and pled guilty. He was sentenced to life with the possibility of parole in ten years.

In 2003, Luis Hidalgo, Jr., took over the club. Along with his son, Luis Hidalgo III, and his girlfriend, Anabel Espindola, he made some changes. One of them was an all-male nude act known as "the Palomino Stallions." This, he reasoned, would bring in more female customers. Two years later, the booze was still flowing, and the nude dancers were still strutting their stuff. Forty-four-year-old Timothy "TJ" Hadland went to work at the club as the night doorman. He saw it as a great side gig that supplemented his income and helped with the expense of raising teenagers.

In early May 2005, Hadland quit his job amidst bitter feelings. He did not go quietly and had some unflattering things to say about the club and its owners. Management at the Palomino, he said, was being unfair to the competition by diverting customers away from their establishments. In order to do this, they were paying cabdrivers hefty fees to bring customers to the Palomino.

This cost the Palomino and it infuriated the Hidalgos and Espindola when they heard about it. These were not the sort of people who sat down and discussed their differences. Two weeks after he quit the Palomino Club, Hadland's body was discovered on a lonely road near Lake Mead.

He had driven there to meet his friend and former co-worker Deangelo Carroll; he had come for weed. While Hadland came alone in the darkness, Carroll had not. He had three others in the Palomino Club van with him. One of them slipped out of the van and shot Hadland in the head as he stood talking to Carroll at the driver's open window.

They had carried out the $5,000 contract. Leaving Hadland's lifeless body with Palomino Club ads scattered around it, Carroll spun the van around and headed back to Las Vegas. In their haste to get away from the scene, none of the four men thought to check Hadland's cell phone, which was left on the front seat of his car. Deangelo Carroll was his last call, and it did not take long for investigators to come knocking at his door.

Criminals tend to turn on each other like cannibals when the heat is on. Deangelo Carroll, Anabel Espindola, and Kenneth Counts were true to form. They sought deals in exchange for talking. The Hidalgos hired Dominic Gentile, one of Las Vegas's top attorneys, and prepared to fight the charges against them. Attorney fees are steep. In order to pay Gentile, the Hidalgos sold the Palomino to him in exchange for legal services.

In 2007, two years after the murder of Hadland, Luis Hidalgo, Jr., and Luis Hidalgo III were each sentenced to twenty years to life imprisonment with the possibility of parole. They would unsuccessfully appeal the sentence in 2012. In exchange for her guilty plea of voluntary manslaughter with a deadly weapon and her testimony, Anabel Espindola was released for time served. Deangelo Carroll was sentenced to life imprisonment with the possibility of parole. Kenneth Counts, the actual shooter, was convicted of conspiracy to commit murder and sentenced to an eight-to-twenty-year sentence. Dominic Gentile sold the Palomino Club to his son, Adam, who still operates it.

Little Mouse

Long before the mob, the slots, and the showgirls, there was Little Mouse. His hideout was in what is known today as the Valley of Fire State Park, which is 52 miles north of Las Vegas. One of the favorite spots for visitors to this 46,000-acre park is Mouse's Tank. Named for a Paiute who went by the name Little Mouse, it is a hidden area inside a rock formation in Petroglyph Canyon. Clever Little Mouse had the perfect location to ensure that he would never go without water while hiding from the law. He quenched his thirst by drinking rainwater that was held in a depression of the rock. Food was a different matter.

When he was hungry, Little Mouse came down into the valley and stole whatever he wanted from farmers and miners. There are many different versions of the story of Little Mouse and the crimes he committed. According to one tale, Little Mouse was a law-abiding man who worked as a ferryman on the Colorado River, but he had one big character flaw—he liked to drink, and he lost his job because of his outlandish behavior when he was drunk.

So he came to this area and stole from others. Hunger, according to the story, was Little Mouse's undoing. One July morning in 1890, he came down from the Valley of Fire to forage for food. After stealing from a farmer, Little Mouse got angry when the farmer demanded payment. He shot and killed the man, then shot two prospectors who stood between him and freedom.

Anxious to get back to the safety of his hiding place, he did not know that an angry posse had picked up his trail and were following him back to the Valley of Fire. When they caught up with him, Little Mouse realized there was no escape. The men surrounded him and demanded that he surrender; Little Mouse decided he would not be taken alive. He pulled his gun and fired wildly. The posse opened fire, putting an end to the legend of the renegade Paiute who had avoided apprehension for so long out in the unforgiving desert.

The Lawless Eldorado Canyon

Nelson is all but a ghost town located in Eldorado Canyon about 42 miles south of Las Vegas. Very few people live here today. It was here that the Techatticup Mine was formed in the 1870s. Over the next seventy years, the Techatticup would become one of Nevada's richest producers with more than $250 million in gold, silver, and ore being pulled from the mine.

The discovery of gold and silver at the Techatticup Mine brought hundreds of people pouring into the Eldorado Canyon. At that time, there were more people living here than there were living in the Vegas Valley. It was a violent area of disillusioned men who had either fought in, or deserted, during the Civil War looking to strike it rich, and thieves and murderers who came in search of easy pickings. Then too, there were the Native American Paiute and Cocopa, some of which resented the white man taking over here on the edge of the Colorado River.

John Nash came to the Eldorado Canyon with big ideas. He took on three partners in his mining claim, paid them $5,000 dollars each, and then tricked them into killing each other. Two of the men died of strychnine poisoning; the other was shot to death. His partners were all dead, but the scheme did not quite work out the way Nash had hoped. He slowly went mad with the idea that one of the dead partner's ghosts followed him wherever he went.

Avote, a young Paiute who lived in Eldorado Canyon deeply resented the takeover of the region by the white man and vowed to make it his mission to rid the canyon of as many as he could. In 1897, he killed Charles Nelson, a mining leader who operated a small boat landing and port on the Colorado River, and for whom Nelson was named. People were outraged. They demanded something be done to stop Avote.

In keeping with the Paiute custom, the duty of bringing his murderous relative to justice fell to Avote's seventeen-year-old brother, Queho. Eventually, Queho would kill more people than Avote ever had. Yet on this day, he set out to stop his murderous brother, following his trail for several hours. They met up with each other on Cottonwood Island.

Whatever he may have wanted, there was nothing Queho could do but execute the wrongdoer. Either Avote would die or the whole tribe would die. So Queho shot Avote. To prove that the sentence had been carried out, he cut off his brother's hand and returned it to the white men. Another version of this story has Queho cutting off Avote's head and carrying it back to Nelson in a burlap bag. Some claim that Avote was not a murderer, but a convenient scapegoat the real killer hid behind. There may some truth to this judging by the many murders Queho later committed.

Queho is often described as Nevada's first mass murderer. He was born about the same time that the infamous Mouse of the Valley of Fire took his own life when surrounded by a sheriff's posse. Like Mouse and Avote, there would be so many tales told about him; the truth was so blurred and often difficult to find at all. The only common thread running through all these stories is bad luck. Queho was an orphan whose mother died shortly after giving birth to him and he never knew his father whose identity remains a mystery. Queho was raised by his mother's relatives at the Paiute reservation in Las Vegas and because of a deformity was not accepted by the others. In the superstitious world in which he lived, a deformity was considered a bad omen. Some stories claim it was Queho's club foot that set him apart and made him an outcast. Others say his right leg was noticeably shorter than his left.

If records are to be believed, Queho became a serial killer with at least twenty-three deaths on his hands—men, women, and children; it did not matter to Queho. He knew the area around the canyon better than any living man. Each time there was an unsolved murder, Queho got the blame. Lawmen came searching for him but left empty-handed. After committing his crimes, Queho would take refuge in the rocks and caves. He could always wait them out.

In 1919, Maud Douglas, the wife of a local miner, was found shot to death in her cabin. The blame fell on Queho in spite of the fact that a youngster living with the Douglases claimed that he had witnessed Maud's husband kill her.

Aside from Avote, Queho had a brother named Steve Tecope, who lived within the confines of the law until July 27, 1931, when he shot and killed a man in Searchlight for no apparent reason. Convicted of the crime, Tecope was sentenced to life in prison for the murder. If only Queho could be so easily captured and imprisoned. Disgruntled lawmen retreated back to Las Vegas and gave up on ever finding Queho. Numerous stories went around the city; Queho was long gone and living far from the region. Queho, they said, was living in Las Vegas and walking the streets, free as a bird. Another tale had Queho's ghost hovered over the canyon, taunting all those who had ever chased him. It seemed that every day brought a different tale. Then, one day in 1940, the mystery of Queho was solved.

On a warm February morning, three prospectors were working along a steep cliff high above the Colorado River in the Black Rock Canyon when one of them discovered a low stone wall near a spot some 2,000 feet above the river. Gazing down into the canyon far below, he told himself that this would be a perfect hideout. From this vantage point, a person could see in all directions. He called for his friends to come and see what he had discovered. As the men explored further, they discovered a small cave with tripwire running across it. Why on earth, they wondered, would someone set up a crude alarm system at the cave's entrance?

Their prospecting forgotten, the men crept inside the cave where they found the mummified remains of a man. Huddled up in a fetal position, the man had apparently died a very painful death. The dead man's personal effects were scattered around the cave. These items included several pairs of eyeglasses and shoes, an assortment of weapons, and the badge of a night watchman from the Gold Bug Mine.

Had the infamous Queho been found at last? The debate was on. The Las Vegas chief of police and the coroner went to the cave for a look-see. Some believed it was a snake bite that did Queho in, but the coroner conducting an inquest on the spot said that Queho died of natural causes and not a rattler. They were so certain of the corpse's identity that the chief of police would later admit to kicking it in the behind, something he had waited long years to do.

That was only the beginning of a long line of indignities the mummified Queho would endure. The remains were put on display in the Clark county courthouse where the ghoulishly curious could come and take a peek. When interest waned, the dead Queho was taken to a local mortuary; three years later he was still there. The Las Vegas chief of police agreed to pay the mortuary its fees and gave the mummified Queho to the Las Vegas Elks, who put him on display during the big Helldorado festivities.

In the 1950s, someone stole Queho's bones and scattered them in Bonanza Wash; hopefully Queho, or what was left of him, would not stay here forever. It was not to be. Somehow, Queho's bones were rediscovered and sold to a local Pahrump man for $100. At long last, the old renegade's remains were finally buried

2
WRONG PLACE, WRONG TIME

Sniper at the Mandalay Bay

Las Vegas is a *quid pro quo* city, especially as far as casino hotels go. The person who spends the most receives the most. High-roller Stephen Paddock was at the top of the heap. The sixty-four-year-old high-stakes gambler enjoyed *carte blanche* at his favorite Las Vegas casino hotels. He owned a home in Mesquite, 82 miles northeast of Las Vegas, and another one in Reno. His homes, although they were in comfortable upper middle-class neighborhoods, were not luxurious. Paddock spent little time in either of them. He preferred staying in casino hotels, where he was closer to the action. His room, meals, and drinks were all comped. During some gambling sessions, he would easily drop over $100,000. The former auditor and real estate businessman had the money and could well afford it.

Paddock checked into the Mandalay Bay on September 25. He was on the thirty-second floor, facing the strip. Four days later, Paddock changed his room to 32-134, also on the thirty-second floor, also facing the strip. A week earlier, he had sent his longtime girlfriend back to the Philippines, wired her $100,000 to buy herself a home there, and wished her well—*Paalam aking pagmamahal.*

Now he would enjoy the good life alone or in the company of a prostitute, and he was living it all through a Valium and alcohol haze. When he was not gambling, Paddock was traveling to his home in Mesquite, to other locations in Las Vegas and buying firearms. From September 2016 to October 2017, he purchased over fifty-five guns. With bump stocks attached to his rifles, they could fire in rapid succession, making his weapons all the more deadly.

The first day of October 2017 was typical; it was still hot in Las Vegas. By noon, it would be 90 degrees. Fall's welcome relief had yet to settle on the valley. Tourists from colder climes knew this and loved this about Las Vegas. The Route 91 Harvest Festival was in town for its annual three-day event. The country western festival had been a part of Las Vegas entertainment since its inception in 2014. As with the other years, the event was being held at the Las Vegas Village concert venue, a 15-acre open-air site across from the Luxor and the Mandalay Bay. The popular event, which offered a general admission pass for all three days, went for $210 per person. Over 20,000 tickets quickly sold out.

Headliners included Jason Aldean, who had appeared at the first festival back in 2014. That day was the last day of the three-day event. The site was crowded with over 22,000 concertgoers. Excitement was in the air. At 10.05 p.m., the last singer, Jason Aldean, was onstage and finishing his sixth song of his set, "When She Says Baby." Suddenly, there was the sound of fireworks, but there was nothing in the sky—it was gunfire they were hearing, so Aldean stopped singing. He and his band managed to get off the stage and to safety. The smell of blood and death hung in the air. Concertgoers panicked. They start screaming, pushing, and shoving as they wildly sought refuge from the deadly onslaught. Struck by bullets, people dropped dead throughout the crowd.

Five minutes later, it was all over. Fifty-eight people were dead and 851 were injured. This was the deadliest mass shooting in modern U.S. history, and no one knows why. What demons drove Paddock to commit such a horrendous act? There are no answers. We know that he did it, we know when, and we know where, but we will never know his reasons for having done so. For all its problems, Las Vegas is a big-hearted city. This was never more evident than the days and weeks following this tragedy.

The words "Vegas Strong" were everywhere. The city would not forget those who perished, nor would Las Vegas forget those whose lives were torn apart with the loss of loved ones, or those dealing with terrible injuries.

Crowds gathered at the famous "Welcome to Las Vegas" sign to pay their respects to place flowers and mementos to the memories of lives cut short. In the art district, the names of those lost were memorialized by paintings and rocks.

A year later, a young couple, Todd Wienke and Oshia Collins-Waters, returned to Las Vegas to get married. They would never forget, but they chose the date in order to associate it with happiness and hope rather than the tragedy that had been seared into their brains. They were on a date the night Paddock opened fire on those attending the event. Wienke was shot three times while shielding Collins-Waters from the bullets. They had fallen in love, and now they were man and wife.

In the face of tragedy, Las Vegas maintains a small-town, we-are-one attitude. Vegas really is a big-hearted city. It was recently announced that the MGM Resorts International will convert the Vegas Village venue to a community and athletic center and a parking lot. Included in the plans will be a memorial to the victims of one man's madness.

Death on the Strip—Ammar Harris

Ammar Harris was a show-off. Although he had never been convicted of being a pimp, the twenty-five-year-old liked to boast about his wealth, cars, girls, and pimp lifestyle on social media. People who did not know Ammar Harris very well were impressed, but not everybody was impressed with him.

On February 21, 2013, Harris was leaving the Haze nightclub at the Aria casino around 3.30 a.m., when he and Kenneth Cherry, Jr., got into a heated argument at the valet area. As he pulled his Range Rover out into the heavy strip traffic, Harris was still angry when he saw Cherry get into a Maserati.

Minutes later, Ammar Harris's pulled up alongside Cherry, Jr.'s Maserati at a stoplight on the Strip. Harris glared at Cherry, who did not seem to notice him. Harris turned and looked at his girlfriend Yesenia Alfonso in the passenger seat. Neither of them spoke. Then he turned back and pointed his gun at Cherry and fired three shots, killing him instantly and injuring his passenger. The Maserati spun out of control crashing into a taxi that exploded in a fireball, killing the driver and the passenger of the cab.

Harris and Alfonso fled Las Vegas and headed to Los Angeles the next day. Later, Yesenia Alfonso would say she fled with Ammar Harris only because she was so in love with him. After a weeklong manhunt, Harris was arrested in Southern California and returned to Las Vegas.

On February 26, 2014, almost a year to the day that Ammar Harris shot and killed aspiring rapper Kenneth Cherry, Jr., and causing the death of two other people, he was sentenced to sixteen years for rape and robbery of an eighteen-year-old woman. His jury in the murder case would not hear about this trial and its outcome.

Witnesses for the prosecution included Harris' ex-girlfriend, Yesenia Alfonso, who apparently was no longer in love with him. The defense claimed Harris had endured a terrible childhood that included sexual abuse and poverty. The jury was not sympathetic. It took them less than two hours to decide the fate of Ammar Harris. He appealed his death sentence to the Nevada Supreme Court, but it was upheld. Now, he waits on Nevada's death row.

Senseless

Like the 1930s bank-robbing killers Bonnie and Clyde and the 1950s murderers Raymond Fernandez and Martha Beck, Jerad and Amanda Miller formed a coldblooded killing duo. Unlike the aforementioned killers, the Millers did not commit their crimes out of greed. They were angry, and all that pent-up anger was focused on the government and authority.

Jerad Miller commented on social media:

We can hope for peace. We must, however, prepare for war. We face an enemy that is not only well funded, but who believe they fight for freedom and justice. Those of us who know the truth and dare speak it, know that the enemy we face are indeed our brothers.... To stop this oppression, I fear, can ... only be accomplished with bloodshed.

Amanda Miller commented on social media:

To the people in the world ... your lucky I can't kill you now but remember one day I will get you because one day all hell will break lose and I'll be standing in the middle of it with a shot gun in one hand and a pistol in the other.

Jerad Miller had a long criminal record. Amanda, his wife of two years, had no criminal record. Both were known as anti-government, cop-hating racists. Shortly before noon on Sunday June 8, 2014, Las Vegas Police officers Igor Soldo and Alyn Beck sat down to eat their lunch at a Cici's pizza restaurant. Officer Soldo had been with the department eight years and Officer Alyn Beck had been with the department thirteen years. At forty-one years of age, Beck was ten years older than Soldo, who had come to the United States from Bosnia as a child. Both men were married with kids. They were partners; the conversation this day was easy as theirs always were.

Without warning, the day went sideways. Jerad and Amanda Miller came charging through the door yelling, "This is the start of the revolution!" Jerad Miller cold-bloodedly shot Soldo in the back of the head then turned and shot Beck in the throat.

As the downed officer tried desperately to draw his weapon, both Millers opened fire on him. They then covered the bodies with a yellow "Don't Tread on Me" flag and a swastika. A hastily scribbled note that read "this is the beginning of the revolution" was also left with the bodies.

The two killers stole the dead officers' weapons then ran to a nearby Walmart. Yelling at customers to leave the store, they took up positions in the rear of the building. Amanda shot and killed an armed man who tried to stop Jerad. Police swarmed the building and a gun battle quickly ensued. Like Bonnie and Clyde, Jerad and Amanda Miller went down in a hail of bullets. Jared Miller died first. When she realized the hopelessness of her situation, the injured Amanda Miller put a gun to her head and pulled the trigger.

"The Clark County District Attorney Report on Use of Force Legal Analysis Surrounding the Deaths of Jerad and Amanda Miller on June 8, 2014," states that the incident in Walmart lasted twenty-four minutes. During this time, the Millers fired twenty-nine shots and the police officers only sixteen. Toxicology report indicated that Jared Miller had marijuana in his blood; Amanda Miller did not. Five lives (including those of the two killers) were senselessly lost on a hot summer day in June.

Murder on Aisle One

On Thursday, June 3, 1999, she had a bad feeling about it. When the agency called her with an outcall dance, she did not want to do it, but no one else was available and she really did need the money. So the outcall dancer agreed to take it. Still feeling uneasy, she went to the address supplied and knocked on the door of the small apartment. It was almost 4 a.m.

He opened the door and she stepped in. His eyes were the first thing she noticed. They were cold, cruel, and dead. Without warning, he grabbed her by the hair of the head and threw her to the floor. She was handcuffed and a wide band of tape was placed across her mouth. Zane Floyd then tore her clothing off and violently raped her. After, he shoved her away telling her that this was just one of his sick little fantasies. He raped her again. Then he showed her his .12- gauge shotgun and a bullet, saying, "This one has your name on it."

She felt a chill run up her body. Was she going to die tonight, she wondered. "I'm going to kill the next nineteen people I see," he boasted before raping her again. Fearing for her life, the dancer did not dare argue with him. She was here in his home because Zane Floyd's girlfriend had stormed out of the apartment after an argument. This would be a night the young woman would never forget. Her attacker had stayed up all night drinking and wondering where his life was headed. At twenty, he had enlisted in the Marine Corps, hoping he could turn his life around. It had not worked out the way he hoped it might. After spending four years in the military, Floyd was honorably discharged. He had been back in Las Vegas for a year now.

College had fizzled. He was working as a bouncer at a local sports bar and had recently moved out of his apartment and into this little apartment in back of his parents' house. He was his parents' only child, and like parents everywhere, they had tried to do their best for their son, but he was different. They had taken Floyd for counseling at thirteen and he was put on Ritalin, which seemed to help with his attention deficit disorder. Yet it could not make Zane Floyd whole; nothing could.

He raped her one last time, then shoved her aside and began dressing in his camouflage clothing. She let herself think that if she were lucky tonight, she just might escape with her life. He grabbed her and pushing her toward the door he said, "Get out! Walk west on Oakey."

The outcall dancer was very lucky. Zane Floyd had more important things to take care of. He wanted to know what it felt like to kill someone. She ran out the door and down the street, in the direction he had told her to go; hopefully, she would never again hear from or see this mad man. He pulled a bathrobe over his clothing to hide the shotgun and stepped out the front door and started walking east on Oakey Blvd.

Everyone who knew Zane Floyd described him as a nice guy, but they did not know the man who had just repeatedly raped a young woman so severely she would have nightmares for years to come. They did not know the man dressed in camouflage carrying a .12-gauge shotgun, who calmly walked toward the neighborhood Albertsons grocery store on W. Sahara, which was only two blocks from his home; his parents shopped there. They knew many of the people who worked at the store. The store, like a lot of Las Vegas businesses, was a 24–7 establishment. It never closed. Three separate shifts of employees kept the business going.

It was right around 5 a.m. All across the city, day shifters were up and getting ready to greet the day. Those who worked swing shift were either fast asleep or seriously thinking about sleep, and graveyard workers were counting down the last hours of their shift. This would be the shift of employees Zane Floyd would encounter at Albertsons. Five people who loved, and were loved, and only wanted to live: Thomas Darnell, Chuck Leos, Dennis Sargeant, Zachary Emenegger, and Lucy Tarantino. Zane Floyd took that away from four of them; only Zachary Emenegger would survive.

Floyd strode through the front door, throwing off the bathrobe. Thomas Darnell was at the front of the store arranging grocery carts. Floyd raised the shotgun. Darnell would be the first to die. A bookkeeper, who had just come to work, heard the gunshot and peeped out the window of her office on the second floor. After seeing Zane race through the check stand, the shotgun held menacingly, she ran to the manager's office and called 911.

At the sound of gunshots, customers scampered in search of a hiding spot. Floyd stormed up and down the aisles, shooting anyone he encountered. Chuck Leos and Dennis Sargeant were shot at point-blank range. Some employees hid in the air-conditioning compressor room; others and a customer took cover in the produce cooler. Two hid in the bakery's freezer. In the produce section, Zachary Emenegger attempted to hide from Zane Floyd. Shot twice in the back, he dropped to the floor and pretended to die.

"Yes, you're dead," Floyd said, kicking Emenegger in the side. As he lay there motionless and terrified, Emenegger heard Lucy Tarantino in the bakery pleading with the killer to spare her life. A gunshot silenced her. The rampage lasted only five minutes, but it seemed like a much longer timespan to those who had hidden from the crazed killer.

Metro officers surrounded the store. There was no place for Zane Floyd to run. He came out the front door with the gun at his head. Rather than shoot him, police convinced him to drop his weapon and turn himself in. Later, he would confess to detectives.

> I've always wanted to know, call me crazy, psychotic, whatever, I've just always wanted to know what it's like to shoot someone ... ever since I was a little kid, I've always, you know, ever since I saw my first, my first war movies, I've always just wanted to go to war and kill people.

For the first-degree murders, Floyd was sentenced to death. He appealed the death sentence at the Nevada Supreme Court in 2010, claiming a list of reasons that he was incapable of premeditation: fetal alcohol spectrum disorder, attention deficit hyperactivity disorder, dissociative disorder, and his long-term use of drugs, alcohol, and methamphetamines. He lost the appeal and remains on death row.

Death at the Company Picnic—Anthony Wrobel

Tokes (known elsewhere as gratuities) are the lifeblood of casino gaming employees. Tokes enable gaming service industry employees to enjoy life's extra niceties. When tokes are skimpy, nothing is right. Lifestyles get cramped as budgets get tightened. New rules that affected tokes at the table games had recently been implemented at the Venetian Casino Resort. Card dealer Anthony Wrobel was among those who were not happy with the new rules.

The Venetian Casino Resort was having its company picnic at Sunset Park on April 15, 2018. It was meant to be a good time for all employees, and it was a chance to get out of uniform and mix with people in other departments. This included the executives that many employees knew only by name. Day shifters might have caught a glimpse of them from time to time, but swing shift and graveyard employees probably had not.

Mia Banks, vice president of casino operations, was in attendance. She had been with the Venetian since it opened in 1999. Hector Rodriguez, executive director of table games, was at the picnic table with Ms. Banks near the gazebo area. It was nearing 6 p.m., and the party was just about over; many of the picnickers had packed up and gone home when Anthony Wrobel drove up.

Witnesses said he asked where the bosses were sitting and headed straight for them when told where they were. He stood there at their table a moment before pulling his gun. Eyewitnesses named Anthony Wrobel as the shooter. Mia Banks was pronounced dead at the Sunrise Hospital Medical Center. Gravely injured, Hector Rodriguez told detectives that Anthony Wrobel had shot them.

Wrobel fled town and was later apprehended in Texas and was extradited back to Nevada where he pleaded not guilty. Set to stand trial in October 2019, Wrobel did some thinking and changed his mind. The death penalty was a real possibility if he were to be found guilty, and so he changed his plea to guilty. On November 21, 2019, with victim Hector Rodriguez and the daughters of his victim Mia Banks looking on, he was sentenced to thirty-eight years in the Nevada State Prison.

Mirror, Mirror on the Wall

Of all the places you might expect to find a cosmetic surgery center, the back of a tile store is not one of them, but Ruben Matallana-Galvas and his wife, Carmen Torres-Sanchez, were unlicensed practitioners who needed a place that was easily accessible where not so many questions would be asked. Thus, the back of a Las Vegas tile center is where they set up their unlicensed cosmetic surgery center. No business is successful without customers, so Matallana-Galvas and Torres-Sanchez advertised their cosmetic procedures in local beauty salons. It worked. No one asked to see their licenses. No one asked why they were not practicing in more conventional locations; no one asked because their prices were so affordable.

Like it or not, Las Vegas is a town of the haves and the have nots, and everyone wants to be beautiful, handsome, and gorgeous. Like Hollywood,

Las Vegas is the land of the beautiful. Toned bodies, youth, and beauty are valued above everything else (except for money, of course). Beauty and youth are essential to one's getting ahead; without it, you can forget it.

The haves find it much easier to put down the cash for beauty enhancement than those who struggle to make ends meet in the casino hotels. It is all about the cash, or lack thereof. Everyone wants to be beautiful, though not everyone can afford the high cost of beauty; you are as beautiful as your paycheck permits you to be. Reasonable prices are the reason forty-two-year-old Elena Caro sought out the services of Matallana-Galvas and Torres-Sanchez in the first place.

The French have a saying *"Il faut souffrir pour être belle,"* which translates to "one must suffer to be beautiful." Every woman knows this to be true. Waxing eyebrows is one thing, but what happens when the suffering becomes deadly as it did in the case of Elena Caro?

Elena Caro only wanted a more rounded and youthful backside. To perform her butt enhancement, Caro chose the cosmetic surgery center she had used before—the one in the back of the tile store. Caro had first met Matallana-Galvas and Torres-Sanchez when she went to them to have a few facial wrinkles smoothed via injections. There were no side effects or problems with the procedure. She looked in the mirror and was pleased. She liked her smoother, younger-looking face. Within a few days, her attention wandered to her butt and she was making arrangements to improve it.

On April 9, 2010, she arrived at the tile store for her scheduled appointment. She was given an anesthetic and injected with a gel-like substance. Yet something went terribly wrong. Elena Caro suffered a fatal allergic reaction to the anesthetic. Rather than call 911 for her, Matallana-Galvas and Torres-Sanchez left their patient and made a run for it. Somehow, Elena Caro managed to walk out of the store. She made it as far as the corner of Pecos Road and Lake Mead Boulevard, where she begged passersby for help. An ambulance was summoned but it was too late for Elena Caro. She was pronounced dead on arrival at the hospital.

Matallana-Galvas and Torres-Sanchez packed up cash and a few belongings and sped to McCarran International Airport where they purchased two one-way tickets back home to Colombia. They might have made it, if metro had been a bit slower. Luckily, they were not. They were nabbed at the boarding gate and taken to jail.

The pair pleaded guilty to involuntary manslaughter, conspiracy, and practicing medicine without a license. In October, they appeared before Clark County District Court Judge Abbi Silver and tearfully pleaded for leniency. Judge Silver had little sympathy for the pair. They were each fined $12,000 and given the maximum sentence allowable of up to eight years in prison for their part in Elena Caro's death.

Manicurist

She had her manicure done on December 29, 2018, and her nails looked fantastic, but when it was time to pay for services rendered, she did not have enough cash. She handed the manicurist her credit card. It was refused again and again. Telling the manicurist she was going to her car for money, the customer dashed out the door and attempted to drive away. The manicurist had been stiffed before. She knew the game, so she ran after her patron and jumped in front of the car, while her husband held tightly to the back of the car. She lost her grip and fell to the ground.

The patron was a young woman with nice nails and no qualms. She panicked, pressed the gas pedal and drove over Ngoc Quynh Nhu Nguyen, the manicurist killing her. All for a $35 dollar manicure.

She fled the state and was later arrested in Arizona. Her attorney asked for her to be placed on house arrest until her trial. In denying the request, Clark County District Court Judge Douglas Herndon said that proof is evident that she was involved in a homicide. At time of writing, Krystal Whipple is awaiting trial in the Clark County Detention Center.

3
UNSOLVED

The Death of Archibald Stewart

In 1855, Mormon leader Brigham Young sent William Bringhurst and thirty missionaries to settle this region in the furthest reaches of the Utah territory on the edge of the Mojave Desert. They built a fort (the old Mormon Fort) that was little more than an adobe walled enclosure and planted their crops, which would be irrigated by water from the creek and the nearby springs. The blistering desert climate proved too much for the settlers who abandoned the site after only two years.

Ten years later, Octavius D. Gass, encouraged by his good friend Conrad Kiel, bought the old Mormon Fort and surrounding acreage and began ranching in earnest near Kiel's ranch, but Gass was neither a good rancher nor a businessman. He quickly ran out of money and borrowed $5,000 from Pioche rancher Archibald Stewart. As collateral on the loan, Gass offered up his ranch. The interest rate was steep. Sixteen years later, Gass was unable to repay the loan. Stewart took over the ranch and moved his family onto it. For this, he incurred the wrath of his neighbor Conrad Kiel, who insisted that Stewart had swindled his friend out of his ranch. The enmity between the Kiels and the Stewarts would last a lifetime.

After much debate and political wrangling, the 7-acre Kiel Ranch Historic Park in the City of North Las Vegas is a reality. It is all that remains of the old Kiel Ranch, which encompassed more than 200 acres. It was here on July 13, 1884, that Archibald (Archie) Stewart was murdered. Sixteen years later, Conrad Kiel's two sons—Edwin and William—would also be shot down and killed at this location. Archibald Stewart, Edwin Kiel, and William Kiel were the victims of Las Vegas's first unsolved murders. To this day, none of the three murders has been solved.

Central to this story was Archibald Stewart's widow, Helen. Known as the "First Lady of Las Vegas," Helen Stewart played an important part in early day Las Vegas history. In 1892, she became the first appointed postmaster of Las Vegas, and in 1916, she was the first woman elected to the Clark County School District's Board of Trustees, and the first woman to serve on a Las Vegas jury. All this happened long before women were given the right to vote.

The 1884 murder of her husband altered the direction of Helen Stewart's life forever. As a young bride in Stockton, California, she probably envisioned a life similar to what other women of her era were living, but it all changed one day in that long-ago July.

In July 1884, she would not keep it from her husband. When he returned home, Helen Stewart told him about the malicious lies Schyler Henry, a former ranch hand of theirs, was spreading about her. Henry had come to her to quit and demanding to be paid severance, while Archie was away on business. She knew nothing about ranch hand pay, much less what was owed to Schyler Henry, and so she refused to pay him. Henry angrily cursed at her and left the ranch that afternoon. He went to work at Conrad Kiel's ranch and continued to tell lies about Helen Stewart.

Archibald Stewart was hot-headed; he would not allow such lies to sully his wife's reputation. He would demand that Schyler Henry take his vicious lies back. Early the next day, Steward still wild with fury, grabbed his rifle, saddled his horse, and headed for the Kiel ranch about 1 mile north. Helen Steward watched the horse gallop into the distance, hoping that she had done the right thing, hoping this was not something she would regret for the rest of her life.

The sun moved overhead as the afternoon wore on. Another sweltering day in the desert, Helen Stewart and her children sat in the shade of the porch. No one ever grew accustomed to this heat. Heavy into her fifth pregnancy, Helen wondered what was keeping her husband. She shifted in her chair and watched as a horse came galloping toward the house. The horse stopped at the porch and the rider quickly slid from the saddle. Silently, he handed her a neatly folded piece of paper, remounted, and turned toward the Kiel Ranch. She unfolded the paper and stared at it in disbelief. "Mrs. Stewart send a team and take Mr. Stewart away. He is dead. C. Kiel."

She left the children with a caretaker and saddled her horse. With a ranch hand following in the spring wagon, she raced toward the Kiel Ranch. There, she found her husband's lifeless form covered by a heavy woolen blanket and lying in the dirt. She took him home and buried him in a coffin made from the doors of their house. She vowed to stay on the ranch and see that justice was done.

A month passed. The grand jury was convened in Pioche to the north; its verdict of self-defense would be a bitter disappointment to Mrs. Stewart, but this would not defeat her. She would go on to successfully raise her children and to become a well-respected businesswoman and historian. In 1886, she married her former ranch-hand Frank Roger Stewart, who was not related to Archibald Stewart. As long as she lived, the memory of finding her husband Archibald Stewart under a blanket at the Kiel Ranch would haunt Helen Stewart.

While Conrad Kiel had sworn that Archibald Stewart was shot in self-defense, Helen Stewart knew that Kiel's ranch was a haven for men who flouted the law. She believed her husband's murder was a well-planned ambush that had been carried out by Conrad Kiel and his ranch hand, Hank Parrish. Eventually, fate would eventually catch up with them.

On December 16, 1890, the *White Pine News* carried the following story that surely gave Helen Steward some closure:

Hank Parish, for the murder of A.G. Thompson at Royal City last July, was hung in front of the jail yesterday at noon. The death warrant was read by Sheriff Bassett in the jail, and at two minutes to 12 o'clock the solemn procession wended its way from the jail to the scaffold, Parish ascending the steps without the least apparent fear. There were quite a number of spectators within the inclosure [*sic.*], and Parish stepped to the front railing and addressed them. He said:

"I have been charged with a great many crimes; I killed three men, and I was right in doing it. The last man I killed (Thompson), he assisted in stringing me up three times. They say I have a wife and family that I have not treated right. My wife has been dead thirteen years; I have two children in Oregon, well fixed. I am an ignorant man, have always been persecuted, and am innocent of crime. All this will appear in Mr. Murphy's book of my life, and I want you to believe it."

These words were spoken calmly and with ordinary coolness. He made no reference whatever to the Unknown Realm into which he was about to be launched, nor expressed any regret for anything he had done.

He then stepped back on the trap door, shook hands with the Sheriff and his attendants, the black cap was pulled over his head, the rope adjusted about his neck—and the *News* reporter hurriedly walked into the Court House to prevent witnessing the final act in the drama of life and death.

Sheriff Bassett sprung the trap; the fall was a little over six feet, and the doomed man's neck was broken. There was not a move or a quiver of the body, and as soon as Dr. Campbell could get to feel the pulse he pronounced life extinct. The whole time occupied in the execution was but 12 minutes. Parish went on the scaffold at 2 minutes to 12 and was cut down at 10 minutes past 12.

Dr. Campbell examined his pulse before he left the jail. It was beating at 99. When the black cap was pulled over his head it ran up to 142. That Parish was a bad man, and met the fate he deserved, is the general sentiment of this community.

Ely is approximately 242 miles north of Las Vegas. It was in Ely that Hank Parish was hanged. When noting the execution in her diary, Helen Stewart boldly underlined her words. With the death of Conrad Kiel, her enemies were no more.

Murder at the Kiel Ranch—Las Vegas's First Unsolved

The murder of Edwin and William Kiel has puzzled historians and true crime buffs for over a century. While there is much speculation as to the identity of the killer, the case is no closer to being solved than it was on the day of the murders, October 11, 1900.

Conrad Kiel had been dead six years. With his passing, the bitterness between the Kiels and the Stewarts eased. As they occasionally did, Helen Stewart's second husband, Frank Stewart, and her son, Hiram, rode out to the Kiel Ranch to visit and do business with the Kiel brothers.

The ranch was deathly quiet, making it strange that the sound of their approaching horses had not anyone from the ranch house to greet them. It was the neighborly thing to do. The men dismounted and knocked on the door. When their knock went unanswered, they waited a moment then stepped inside the house, calling to its occupants. Something was not right here. In the kitchen, they discovered Edwin's lifeless body sprawled across the floor; a gunshot wound to the head had cut short his stay on this earth.

The men cautiously backed out the door and started looking for the other Kiel brother, William. The search ended at the irrigation ditch some yards from the house where they found him nearly submerged in the water. William Kiel was as dead as his brother. At his feet was a shotgun. His injuries appeared to be more substantial than those of his brother, with a shotgun wound in the left arm, a second in the chest, and a third bullet lodged near his left eye.

In a letter from Helen Stewart to Justice of the Peace Orr dated the same day as the discovery of the men's bodies, Stewart wrote "it is either a case of murder suicide or both." A coroner's jury later determined that to be the case. They found that Edwin had killed William in a fit of rage; then, they surmised, he became filled with remorse at what he had done and turned the gun on himself.

Still another theory was taking shape among the thirty or so people that lived in the Las Vegas valley at that time. There were those who believed that Hiram Stewart had killed the Kiel brothers as payback for his father's untimely death. Nothing was ever proven. The case was filed as a murder-suicide and closed. Like that of Archibald Stewart, the Kiel brothers' deaths would remain shrouded in mystery.

Edwin and William were buried in wooden coffins beside their father in the family cemetery on the Kiel Ranch. The truth of their deaths seemed destined to be just one more in a string of mysteries. Then, in 1975, came an opportunity to discover some answers in the case of the three deaths. The body of Archibald Stewart was to be exhumed at the site of the old Las Vegas Ranch and the city of North Las Vegas began to expand.

The area in which the old ranches once stood was in the midst of a growing city. History is often forgotten as progress demands that the past makes way for the future and the needs of the living, and if this comes at the expense of the dead, so be it. The dead do not pay taxes and they do not vote.

So the old cemetery was excavated in 1975 and the bodies were exhumed. A distant relative of the Kiels who had given permission for exhumation of the bodies also gave permission for them to be taken to University of Nevada Las Vegas (UNLV) and studied. Dr. Sheilagh Brooks, a forensic anthropologist in the UNLV Anthropology Department set to work and soon discovered that Edwin Kiel was felled by two different weapons. This bears out statements that were made by those who had seen his body shortly before burial.

In the case of the Kiel brothers, Edwin Kiel was vindicated. He had been shot in the back of the neck, thus making suicide impossibility. He had not murdered his brother and then killed himself. William Kiel had died of two shotgun blasts to the face. The angle of his wounds indicated there may have been more than one killer at the Kiel Ranch.

Did the Mob Kill Sonny Liston?

Former world heavyweight boxing champion, Sonny Liston died in 1970 at his home at 2058 Ottawa Drive shortly before New Year's Eve. His wife, Geraldine, who had been out of town for two weeks visiting relatives, grew increasingly worried when all her calls home went unanswered. She flew back to Las Vegas and discovered her husband of fourteen years dead on the king-sized bed the couple shared. The former champ, according to the coroner, died of natural causes. Hardening of the arteries will get you every time, so will heavy heroin use; then too, being on the bad side of some serious mob hitmen will do you in as well.

The coroner found traces of morphine and codeine in his system and some believe Liston was helped out of this world by a fatal overdose administered by mob hitmen. If that was the case, you have to ask yourself why. Word on the street was that Sonny was dealing; he was, but he was strictly small time. No one cared about him hustling a bit of drugs that helped defray the cost of his own drug habit. Those who believe Liston was murdered point to his 1964 heavyweight championship match with Muhammad Ali (then Cassius Clay).

The February 25, 1964, fight, they say, was fixed. When Liston gave up at the beginning of the seventh round, speculation went wild. The FBI investigating the fight found no evidence of a fix. Their next match was in May 1965. By that time, Cassius Clay had changed his name to Muhammad Ali, who knocked Liston out to win the bout in the first round. If Liston had taken a dive, as some believe, his knowledge of the facts surrounding that dive would be dangerous to someone. Six years later, he was an old man with a big drug habit, and he had to be silenced. Was it old age or a mob hitman that finally caught up with Liston? That depends on who you ask.

Tupac

Rapper and actor Tupac Shakur holds a dubious Las Vegas record—he is the only celebrity to have been murdered in the city. September 7, 1996, might have been just another hot day in the desert, yet it was not. Anticipation of a fight billed as the Championship Part 11 had Las Vegas teeming with news media, sports fans, and more celebrities than usual. Those who were not able to attend could watch pay-per-view, which would be shown on Showtime.

Tupac Shakur was a fight fan, and like the others in Vegas this day, he was here to attend the much-touted World Boxing Association heavyweight championship fight between Bruce Seldon and Mike Tyson that was scheduled that evening at the MGM Grand. Before this day ended, the fight would be secondary to an unsolved murder.

Every fight fan in attendance that night would not be happy with this fight. Tyson knocked Seldon to the mat twice, winning the match by a TKO in the first round of the fight. Lasting only a minute and forty-nine seconds, the fight is one of the shortest heavyweight championship fights in boxing history. "Fix, fix, fix," chanted many of those at ringside. Seldon, they believed, had taken a dive, but the fight they had paid big bucks to see was over and the crowd swarmed toward the exits.

Anger and disappointment hung in the air as grumbling fans made their way to the doors. While Shakur and his entourage made their way toward the hotel exit, they ran into gang members from Southern California and a fight ensued. Tupac jumped into the middle of the fight. His friend, Suge Knight, pulled him out of the fracas before security guards arrived to break it up. The two men then drove to Tupac's room where he made a quick change of clothes.

As it was so hot, Tupac Shakur did not bother with his bulletproof vest. The decision would cost him his life. *En route* to Club 662, their party destination, they cruised along with the BMW's sunroof open and the music booming. They were young and having a good time. Ten minutes into the journey, Suge Knight stopped at a red light at the corner of Flamingo and Koval Lane. A white Cadillac pulled up beside the BMW.

Its occupants rolled down their windows and without warning opened fire. Shakur was struck four times. He died at the University Medical Center of Southern Nevada a week later on Friday 13 without ever having gained consciousness. Police have their suspicions, but the murder of Tupac Shakur remains officially unsolved.

4
CASINO HEISTS

Tony Cornero's Stardust Dream

Eight years after Bugsy Siegel's unfortunate exit from Las Vegas's gambling scene, gangster Tony Cornero came to town dreaming an even bigger Las Vegas dream. He had enjoyed earlier Vegas success in 1931 with his Meadows Club, built outside the city limits on Boulder Highway. The Meadows was the first casino built in Las Vegas after the Nevada State Assembly passed Assembly Bill 98 legalizing gambling. Governor Balzar signed the bill into law on March 19, 1931, and Cornero's Meadows Club opened in July.

Suddenly, Tony Cornero was making money, lots of it. He might have continued to do so, if the Lucky Luciano crime family had not come calling with their hands out. They knew that Tony was doing well, and they wanted their share. When they demanded a percentage, Tony refused.

In retaliation, the mob torched the meadows. No one refuses the mob. With his casino in ashes, Cornero took the hint, sold his holdings, and moved back to Southern California. Yet Tony Cornero was not one to give up. He would wait.

He bought a 40-acre parcel on the strip and made plans to build the world's largest casino hotel. He would call it the Stardust. In July 1955, Tony Corner, was a Las Vegas big shot. The middle-aged mobster owned the newest casino hotel, the Stardust, and he was well connected. The way he gambled, few people realized that Tony was broke and desperate. Cost overruns were causing him the same problems Bugsy Siegel had faced a decade earlier. Cornero did not have enough money to stock the Stardust with booze and fill the tills. Without a loan, he would not be able open the casino on time.

He had come here to the Desert Inn begging the mob for a loan, but they knew what a heavy gambler Cornero was. If not for his gambling losses, he would not have money problems. They turned him down. In desperation, Tony took to the craps game; eventually, his losing streak would come to an end.

On Sunday, July 31, 1955, when down $37,000, Tony lost his temper and got into a screaming match with the croupier—a big no-no in any casino, especially one with mob connections. When a cocktail waitress showed up at the table with a tray full of drinks, Cornero grabbed for one and gulped it, thinking a drink might calm him down. He tried not to think about how badly he needed a loan or a big winning streak.

Something was wrong. He grabbed his chest and tumbled to the floor. Dropping dead on the casino floor is bad for business. His lifeless body was quickly moved to a private room, out of sight of the gambling public. Tony Cornero may have been lucky seven years earlier when he opened the front door of his Beverly Hills mansion to armed gunmen. He had barely avoided being murdered like Bugsy Siegel, but luck is a funny thing; sooner or later, it turns, and Tony's luck had run out. On the bright side, Tony no longer had to worry about that loan.

It would be four hours before the coroner was notified. This made some wonder what really killed Tony. If he had been poisoned by some mysterious substance added to his drink, no one would ever know. His glass was whisked away and washed clean. The cocktail waitress, according to some rumors, was given a nice month-long vacation to the destination of her choice.

The coroner's jury found that a coronary thrombosis had conveniently stopped Tony in his tracks, and it was business as usual. There is an old showbiz phrase that states "the show must go on." This is especially true in gambling; time is money, and no one wants to waste it. Tony's dream came true three years later when the Stardust opened under new management and ownership. It is too bad that he was not alive to see it.

The Stardust's $500,000

The Stardust opened in 1958 and operated 24/7 for the next forty-eight years. In that time, the casino was robbed three times. That in itself is amazing, considering how many times a few other casinos have been robbed.

An employee who steals from a casino will eventually get caught. Bill Brennan is probably the one exception. His crime is the stuff of gaming legends. He could be anywhere, this man who calmly walked off shift with $500,000 of the Stardust's dollars never to be seen again. There are those who believe Bill Brennan had an accomplice who killed him, took the money, and split, but that could just be wishful thinking on the part of those who like their casino robberies neatly solved. Maybe they are right that Bill Brennan did not get away and he is not enjoying his ill-gotten gain on some island paradise. If the mob had still been in charge of the Stardust, Bill Brennan would be moldering in some lonely desert grave between Las Vegas and Stateline, but they were not. Nonetheless, it is still possible that was where Brennan ended up.

Brennan was not the first employee to help himself to Stardust cash. Royal Hopper beat him to that in September 1991. Hopper struck twice. The $1 million take was double what Bill Brennan walked away with, but then Hopper got caught.

Both Hopper and Brennan were employees of the Stardust at the time of the robberies. Hopper worked two years as a security guard, sizing up the place and the money procedures before making his move. He also had the help of his son and a friend; they were arrested seven months after the robbery in April 1992, so it slid out of the news quickly. Casinos like it this way; they do not want to advertise their vulnerabilities. Bill Brennan was working in the sportsbook when Hopper committed his robberies. Casino gossip being what it is, news of the Hopper's theft must have raced through the casino faster than even the most fleet-footed Keno runner. Maybe Hopper's robbery gave the thirty-four-year-old Brennan some ideas on how he might increase his net worth funded by his employer.

Then again, maybe Brennan only wanted to see if he could get away with it. He had been employed at the Stardust four years. He knew how the system worked. As bad as he wanted a promotion, his boss had told him that he did not have what it takes to be a supervisor. He took the news well, and although he had not been promoted to supervisor, he was a good and trusted employee. This all changed on Tuesday September 22, 1992, when the good and trusted employee took a lunch break and walked out the door with $500,000 in cash and chips.

Like that of Hopper's robbery, news traveled fast about Bill Brennan, the thief. Casino gossip was that Brennan had fallen in with a smooth-talking high-stakes gambler who convinced him to do the heist, so Bill did the deed. However, once he showed up with all that money, his partner murdered him and made off with the loot. The investigation was handled so swiftly and quietly that some of those working in other casino hotels did not even know about Brennan's theft. Although $500,000 does not go as far as it once did, it took Bill Brennan far enough away so that he was never seen or heard from again.

The statute of limitations had long since passed when the Stardust was imploded fifteen years later on March 13, 2007. Did Bill Brennan know, and did he even care? Odds are, Bill Brennan is as dead as the Stardust, but who knows—maybe one day he will come forward, write a bestselling book about his crime, and appear on all the late-night TV shows to promote it.

The Biker Bandit

In his autobiography *Where the Money Was: The Memoirs of a Bank Robber*, early twentieth-century bank robber Willie Sutton said of robbing banks, "Why did I rob banks? Because I enjoyed it. I loved it." Sutton helped himself to a lot of different banks' money during his forty-year career, which netted him nearly $2 million. Though he denied it, legend has it that Sutton, when asked why he robbed banks, stated, "that's where the money is."

The same can be said for casinos—that is where the money is. This is why casinos occasionally get robbed. However, they try to keep these robberies on the down low. The bold and daring way that Anthony Corleo went about stealing from the Bellagio was newsworthy, and consequently, the story was all over the news.

Although it does not snow in Vegas like it does in other parts of the country, December is traditionally a slow time for the casinos. December 14, 2010, was no exception. Emboldened by OxyContin and cocaine, Corleo arrived at the Bellagio with a plan and a gun. He had already robbed the Suncoast of close to $19,000, so he considered himself somewhat experienced at taking casino money. Clad in dark coveralls, rubber gloves, and a motorcycle helmet with the visor down, he casually strolled through the pit and toward the high-limits craps table and the money.

"Move it!" He yelled, shoveling chips from the table into his backpack. When he was sure he had a nice haul, Corleo ran toward the door and out to his awaiting Suzuki. His getaway was clean. His haul was $500,000. Some people do not know when to leave well enough alone. Corleo was one of them; he was too clever for his own good.

He brazenly went back to the Bellagio a few days later. He had not come to rob the place. This time, he was here to live the life of a high roller. Bankrolled by the casino's own stolen chips, he gambled high stakes. He won and he lost. He dined on exquisite and expensive fare and stayed in a luxurious suite, compliments of the Bellagio. Corleo was a high roller, entitled to and receiving the full high-roller treatment. No expense was spared. No one seemed to realize he was the same man who had robbed the place, and then a poker dealer remembered something—Corleo had once confessed to him a wish to rob a table full of chips.

Anthony Corleo had filed bankruptcy in the past couple of years, and he did have a license to drive a motorcycle. He also had a father (George Assad) who happened to be a sitting judge in Las Vegas. Detectives proceeded carefully but were convinced that he was their man.

A sting was set up and Corleo walked right into it, offering up several of the high-limit chips he had stolen to none other than a Las Vegas metro detective. In a reverse of sins of the father, Corleo's father lost his bid for re-election as a municipal court judge. Anthony Corleo was found guilty and sentenced to nine to sixteen years. He will have a lot of time to think about the error of his ways. However, the next man to rob the Bellagio was not as lucky as Corleo.

Bellagio Cage Cashier Robbery

On Tuesday afternoon, November 28, 2017, wearing a blonde wig and a pair of glasses, the robber, his face concealed by bandages, confidently strode up to the poker room cashier cage, pointed his gun at the cashier, and demanded money. Well-trained, the cashier did not try to dissuade the man. As was casino policy, the money was handed over. The robber walked out the door and got into his nearby getaway car, a silver Chevrolet Cruz. One of those patrons playing poker nearby was actor James Woods, who may have got the drop on news media when he tweeted about the robbery and how cool casino staff had remained during the ordeal. His robbery may not have been as stealthy as that of Anthony Corleo, but the bandaged robber got away with it—for a while.

As it worked so well the first time, convicted felon Michael Cohen stupidly attempted to rob the Bellagio again on March 15, 2019. With his bag of stolen money and chips, he ran out into the valet area, looking for a car. He tried to carjack a woman who refused to open the door for him. Metro police in the area ran toward him. Cohen shot at them. If not for his Kevlar vest, one of the officers would have died in the shootout. The police fired back, hitting Cohen in the heart and killing him. Every gambler knows that luck is a funny thing. Today's lucky winner is tomorrow's unlucky loser. Just when you think you've got a handle of it, your luck can turn sour as Cohen's did. He died right there, with his bag of stolen loot.

The Three Pigs

Their plan probably sounded like a foolproof plot when they hatched it, but the devil was in the details, and you know what they say about best-laid plans. On March 25, 2017, the men were well-dressed, complete with pig masks. They arrived with sledgehammers and hacked their way into a high-end jewelry store at the Bellagio. While one of them stood guard, a cell phone user captured the moment with the phone camera and put it up on social media. How often do you see a porcine in evening attire?

Once their bags were filled with a lot of pricey baubles, the robbers made their way to their getaway car in the parking garage. However, the car would not start. They tried to steal another vehicle; when that did not work out any better, they fled on foot. That was the worst plan of all. The robbers were apprehended, and without going to the market, they were hauled off to jail. There is no word on whether or not they cried "wee, wee, wee," all the way there.

Two Against the House

It is bad enough when a casino gets robbed; it is even worse when an employee is involved in the theft. If you look around, you will see there are safeguards. Cameras are everywhere, likewise security guards, the rules and regulations. While these might deter most would-be criminals, they are seen merely as obstacles to be overcome by the stealthy self-assured thief. It is not always someone coming from the outside to do the cheating. According to the Nevada Gaming Commission, 34 percent of those arrested for robbing or cheating a casino are employees.

Bellagio craps game dealers James R. Cooper, Jr., and Mark M. Branco were like the proverbial foxes in the henhouse. By Las Vegas standards, they were earning a decent living, but it was not enough; they wanted more. They intended to steal what they could and get away with it. Between 2012 and 2014, with a little help from their friends Jeffrey D. Martin and Anthony G. Granito, they managed to cheat their employer out of a little over $1 million.

Craps is basically a dice game. According to those in the know, the craps game offers the second-best odds in casino gambling, just behind blackjack. Seven come eleven—do not get too comfortable with that. The fast-paced game is more complicated than simply rolling dice, making wagers, and winning or losing. The player is merely betting on dice rolls, but there are different types of bets. Cooper's and Branco's scheme involved what was dubbed "phantom hop bets." A hop bet is similar to a hard way bet, except the player gets paid more. The hop bet is high risk. The player is betting on what the next roll of the dice will be. They are to call out what that number will be. Everything takes place under the watchful eye of the boxman (the table supervisor seated behind the casino's chips and between the two dealers and overseeing the paying of all wagers).

Think of the odds for a moment. It was the odds of winning such bets (452 billion to 1) that got Cooper and Branco noticed, watched, and finally caught. After having been arrested and charged, Cooper agreed to testify before the grand jury. He explained that Branco had devised the scheme and that the two had used it twenty years earlier in another Vegas casino. In their phantom bet scheme, the player (either Martin or Granito) would mutter something indistinguishable, in order to appear that a hop bet was in place. When the game was over, the dealer nodded as if the hop bet had won on the particular roll. Thieves may always be dreaming up ways to take advantage of casino weak spots, but casinos are also always finding ways to stop them in their crooked tracks.

Since this time, Vegas crap tables have been redesigned. In the past, there was no place on the table for a hop bet. It was all verbal. Thanks to Cooper and Branco, there is now a distinct place on the table for players to place their hop bets. For their troubles, the four men were sentenced to prison, pay restitution, and have the dubious distinction of having their names placed in Nevada's Black Book (A.K.A. the list of excluded persons); they are never permitted to step one foot into a Nevada casino.

Cameron James Kennedy's Bad Idea

The scheme enacted on January 10, 2018, was both brazen and stupid. He was out on parole and under federal supervision for bank robbery. Nonetheless, Cameron James Kennedy was having trouble staying on the straight and narrow. He decided this might be a good time to try his hand at robbing the New York New York casino. However, there was one problem—that pesky GPS device the feds had fitted him with. All problems have a solution. He carefully cut off the ankle bracelet and lathered his face with black makeup; it was the perfect disguise, or so he thought. At the cashier's cage, he showed his handgun, telling the cashier, "I want all your hundreds, and don't mess around!" He left the casino with $23,000 and hailed a taxi.

It seemed that the disguise had worked. When asked to describe the robber, the cashier did not hesitate. He was an African American, but then the cashier started thinking and decided that the robber's skin tone was too blotchy to be that of an African American. The robber had to have been a white guy in black facepaint.

Kennedy was not stingy. He spent his ill-gotten loot freely. He gave a friend a prepaid debit card. The friend could not help but wonder just how Kennedy had come into the money, so he reported him. Two months after the robbery, Kennedy was arrested and charged with interference with commerce by robbery, and he was right back where he started from.

Reginald Johnson Treasure Island

Reginald Johnson had tried to rob the Treasure Island Casino Hotel twice before. Neither attempt yielded enough to feed a downtown parking meter, so he perfected his technique. His third attempt was in October 2000, and this was to be the charm, or so it is said. Armed and ready for action, Reginald Johnson came through the door of the Treasure Island Casino Hotel with one thing on his mind, and that was money. He meant to help himself to the cash in the casino's cashier cage. His take was $30,000. Yet then he encountered a security guard and shot him. Luckily, the guard was not fatally wounded. He would live to identify Johnson as the shooter, and if that was not enough, there was all that security video of Johnson during the robbery. He was convicted and sentenced to 130 years. If he had been able to keep that $30,000, it would work out to be about $230.76 per year for each of those 130 years. This puts the wages of sin far below the poverty level.

The Big Score

On September 15, 2005, Heather Tallchief returned to Las Vegas and turned herself in at the U.S. District court. She was tired of looking over her shoulder and she wanted to make things right. She had been on the run for twelve years for her part in a 1993 armored car heist. She and her lover made off with $3 million, but after living abroad and having a child, Tallchief changed her mind. She wanted her son to have a normal life. So, leaving her son in the care of her fiancée in Amsterdam, she came back to Las Vegas to face the music. She was alone in her decision as she had split up with Roberto Sollis several years earlier and she had no idea where he was.

A spokesman for the Loomis car company said wryly, "I don't suppose she turned the money in when she turned herself in." He was right; she had not. Presumably, the money is with Roberto Zalaya Sollis (A.K.A. Julius Sauve), wherever he may be.

She was twenty-one years old and living in San Francisco when she met Roberto Sollis, who had recently been paroled for the murder of a security guard during the robbery of an armored truck. Tallchief fell in love with the glib and much-older Roberto Zalaya Sollis and agreed to move to Las Vegas with him. He had a plan whereby they would have all the money they ever wanted. They would commit the perfect crime. Under his tutelage, she would rob an armored truck. All she had to do was get a job as a driver for the Loomis Armored Car Company and the plan was operational.

She got the job, and she had been working as a driver for about a month. Her route took her and her two co-workers to the automatic teller machines (ATMs) of several casinos. She would drive up to the ATMs on one side of the casino, and while they filled the machines, she would circle around to the other side and pick up her two co-workers. On October 1, 1993, Tallchief dropped them off at Circus Circus ATM and sped away with $3 million in cash.

No one suspected anything yet. They thought she was caught in traffic, so they waited. While they did so, Tallchief and Sollis boarded a chartered plane to Denver and made their getaway. They lived on the run together until Tallchief discovered she was pregnant. It was then that she left Sollis for a better life. Roberto Sollis remains at large. Heather Tallchief was sentenced to sixty-three months in federal prison and was paroled in 2010.

Local Man Makes Away with Millions

Anthony Frisco was a local. He had graduated from Valley High School class of 1983, and he and his girlfriend, Misty Smith, pulled a copycat heist ten months after Heather Tallchief drove off with those millions in an armored truck. However, Frisco and Smith did not get as much money as Tallchief and they certainly did not get as far.

On August 9, 1994, it was 107 degrees in the shade, making a perfect day for ice tea on the veranda and, apparently, a perfect day for stealing a truckload of money. It happened shortly before noon at the old Belz Factory Outlet Mall on Las Vegas Blvd. Brinks armored truck driver Misty Smith did not wait for her coworker to return to the truck. Instead, she drove away with $1.8 million and picked up Anthony Frisco.

They dumped the truck and headed for Mexico, but the authorities were quick this time. They tracked Frisco to Costa Rica where they found him with a suitcase stuffed with $1.5 million of the stolen dollars, and it was off to jail he went. Misty Smith did not fare as well. They found her dead in a hotel room two weeks later. Apparently, she had succumbed to severe dehydration—all that money and not one single glass of *agua*.

Frisco pleaded guilty to robbery in 1996. There is a "some people never learn" rest of the story here. A week before Christmas 2009, Frisco was arrested on suspicion of being the "red sharpie bandit" and having committed eleven bank robberies in Orange County, California. The robber was dubbed the red sharpie bandit because all the robbery demand notes were written with a red sharpie.

5
SORRY, NOT SORRY

Black Widow

In Las Vegas, someone is always figuring the odds. Even for a murder, the odds must be astronomical that Las Vegas real estate magnate Ron Rudin would be murdered in the same month (just days before Christmas) and in the same bedroom that his third wife Peggy had died in sixteen years earlier. The similarities end there. Where Peggy's death was at her own hand, Rudin had been murdered.

Rudin had discovered his wife's body. In doing so, he absently picked up the gun she had used to kill herself. Although one of her distraught relatives would later accuse Rudin of killing her, Rudin was never charged with the death of Peggy Rudin, which was ruled a suicide.

Rudin was devastated. Eventually, he started dating again, and he continued to change wives the way most men change socks. When he met Margaret, he had four marriages behind him. By most standards, that made him a poor choice for a husband. Yet then, Margaret also had four failed marriages in her past.

On September 11, 1987, they were married in one of the city's quickie wedding chapels. Ron Rudin moved his bride into his home at 5113 Alpine Place. The arguments soon started. Rudin was self-absorbed and not the faithful husband his new wife had hoped for. He was a player, he was cheap, and he liked his liquor. Still, there was all that money. If she could hang on and wait him out, the money, or a large chunk of it, would be hers.

A year after the marriage, Rudin filed for divorce claiming incompatibility, and Margaret moved out. Several months later, she moved back in and managed to get him to withdraw the complaint. Anxious to know what he was doing at all times, Margaret installed listening devices in his office. Now, she would hear everything he said and to who he said it.

She did not like what she discovered. Ron had a girlfriend, also married. What if this woman should take her place? Margaret wrote an anonymous letter to the woman's daughter. This letter would later be presented as evidence in the prosecution's case against Margaret Rudin.

> Your mother has been screwing Ronald Rudin the realter [*sic*.] for over
> a year. She meets him at vacant houses he owns during her work time …
> and she screws him on dirty carpet floors. He brags to his friends and
> laughs at her because he tells everyone he does not get a motel and he
> does not have to buy her a lunch.

A divorce would be financially devastating, so Ron had to die. He collected guns. The house was a virtual arsenal. She shot him in the same bedroom they had slept together in as husband and wife. When he was dead, she decapitated him and drove his body out to secluded Eldorado Canyon and set it on fire.

Ron Rudin was missing. One day, he was there, and the next, he was not. His anxious employees could not imagine their workaholic boss not showing up for work on time. They called his home only to receive the answering machine. When they finally made contact with Margaret, she seemed unconcerned. She did not know where he was. Two days would pass before they convinced her to file a missing person's report. Within a month, a skull was discovered by campers. Nearby were a burned body and a diamond bracelet bearing the name "Ron."

Ronald Rudin was no longer missing. Margaret Rudin claimed to know nothing, but detectives did not believe her. When forensic investigators came to the house on Alpine in search of evidence, they found plenty; not only were Rudin's tissue and blood spatter on the master bedroom ceiling but so were his first wife Peggy's, after all those years.

Margaret Rudin was charged in the death of Ronald Rudin. Although she maintained her innocence, she fled the state to avoid standing trial. She would be on the run for over two years before they caught up with her in Massachusetts and brought her back to Las Vegas.

In 2001, the titillating trial would be televised; Margaret Rudin would be found guilty and sentenced to life in prison with the possibility of parole after twenty years. Legal maneuvers on Rudin's behalf have continued. Margaret Rudin resides at the Florence McClure Women's Correctional Center in Las Vegas. She will be eligible for parole in two years.

Death of a Bookie

There is a reason Lady Justice is most often depicted as blindfolded. She cares only for the evidence and the facts. The suppositions and what-ifs do not sway her. That said, justice can be fickle, maddening, and frustrating; what one judge sees as perfectly in line with the law, another does not. What one jury finds, a judge can wipe away in a matter of motions and minutes. Never is this more obvious than in cases that involve the death penalty or life without the possibility of parole. Those cases are forever and judges want to get them right. Those that do not can expect that someday, one of their colleagues will do so.

It was at the Mirage that Amy DeChant met Bruce Weinstein at a Texas hold 'em poker table in 1995. The attraction was instant. She moved into his place within the week. Friends and family approved the relationship. Amy ran her own carpet cleaning business and Bruce maintained his sports book operation. Then, things rocked on as long as Bruce was buying Amy expensive gifts.

He was devoted to his mother, Sylvia. They spoke on the phone every day. Then, one day in 1996, he did not call. On July 5, 1996, worried for her son, Sylvia went to the posh southwest Las Vegas home he shared with Amy DeChant. There, she discovered Amy scrubbing the floor and claiming she did not know where the forty-six-year-old Bruce was. In the meantime, Amy DeChant's partner in her carpet cleaning business, Robert Jones, also disappeared.

It would be a month before Sylvia White found out what had happened to her son. On August 11, 1996, a badly decomposed body was discovered by rabbit hunters in a shallow grave off state route 168 near Mesquite. With the discovery of the bookie's body, investigators turned their focus on DeChant and Robert Jones, who had disappeared two days after Weinstein did. It would be almost a year before police finally caught up with him.

Robert Jones was arrested in New Mexico. Once they had one of their suspects safely in custody, investigators called Weinstein's mother with the news. Now all they needed to do was locate Amy DeChant. She would elude detectives until January 1998. It was a sharp-eyed viewer of TV show *America's Most Wanted* that led to her arrest. When she was apprehended at Sunnier Palms Nudist Campground in Port St. Lucie, Florida, DeChant had a story for detectives. She claimed her bookmaker boyfriend, Bruce Weinstein, had been killed by members of the mob, who told her they would not kill her if she cleaned up the mess and kept her mouth shut.

During DeChant's trial, one of the investigators testified that her story about Weinstein being murdered by the mob was a fairy tale. Those words may have stuck in the minds of the nine women and three men on the jury. On October 30, 1998, Nevada would celebrate its official 134th birthday on Halloween the following day; it was also the day jurors reached a decision. After deliberating over fifteen hours in three days, the jury found DeChant not guilty of conspiracy to commit murder but guilty of first-degree murder with a deadly weapon. Her co-defendant and erstwhile boyfriend, Robert Jones, was found not guilty of murder but of being an accessory after the fact.

Sylvia White walked out of the courtroom, feeling that justice had been served. However, that justice was bittersweet, as she told reporters she was going to the cemetery to visit her son. In December 1998, shortly before Christmas DeChant would be given two life sentences without the possibility of parole, Jones was given five years in prison.

Two years later, the Nevada Supreme Court would overturn the convictions, finding that the trial judge erred by permitting the investigator to testify that DeChant's story about the mob hit on Weinstein was a fairy tale. This, found the Supreme Court, unfairly influenced the verdict. Rather than put taxpayers on the hook for another trial, the prosecutors negotiated with DeChant, who would plead guilty to second-degree murder.

"I am accepting this agreement so everyone involved can hopefully find peace and go on with their lives." DeChant said, turning toward Sylvia White; she added, "we both feel a tremendous loss due to Bruce's death."

In 2002, six years after her son's murder, Sylvia White got a taste of law enforcement from the wrong side of a jail cell when Nevada Gaming Control Board agents closed down her illegal sports book operation. The scene of the crime was a rented 1,600-sq. foot home located at 11243 Tribiani Ave. in Summerlin. The landlord did not have a clue that his tenants, White, her grandson, and three partners were operating an illegal sports book operation on the premises.

Their operation was no chump change endeavor. Agents said that they were pulling in several thousand dollars a week in wagers. The seventy-six-year-old White was hit with a slew of charges that included racketeering and operating a sports book without a license. The charges carried heavy fines and some serious jail time for those convicted of them.

After a failed first attempt at parole, Amy DeChant was released from prison in July 2011.

Blast at the Orbit Inn

The scene of the crime is the downtown Container Park in the art district; it is a wonderful place to spend an afternoon or an evening, dining, shopping, listening to music, or just relaxing while enjoying art. This area was different on January 7, 1967. There was no container park with its art and music. This is where the ultra-modern Orbit Inn stood on the corner of 7th and Fremont in downtown Las Vegas. It was here that one of Las Vegas's most spectacular murder–suicides took place. It was a suicide that left torn bodies, rubble, and wreckage in its wake—a suicide that has never been explained.

When twenty-eight-year-old Richard James Parris arrived in Las Vegas with his young wife Christine, he had been AWOL from Fort Ord since November 1966. He realized that sooner or later, the army would catch up with him and off to the stockade he would go. He probably did not care one way or the other. All he had when he checked into the Orbit Inn was a couple pieces of luggage, a gun, and a diabolical plan. Then, too, there were those fifty sticks of dynamite.

He had thought it over and he wanted to end it all, but he did not want to exit this world alone, so the army deserter had an idea. He would take people with him when he went. Parris's victims would include Arizona newlyweds George and Arnell Brooks and Californians John and Lilian Auwaerter. Aside from the six people who were killed, eight people were injured in the bomb blast. No one knows what his motive was. Was Mrs. Parris in on her husband's outlandish plan? Or was she just an innocent victim, unknowingly along for the blast into eternity?

Friends and family were shocked. According to Parris' parents, his and Christine's marriage had been a happy one. Parris and his wife were "very much in love." So why did he kill her, himself, and four other people? Investigators were unable to come up with all the answers. They believed the bombing was the tragic story of a man's love for his wife gone wrong. Maybe he was jealous of her.

Beyond that, there were no explanations, no answers to the question, why. The clerk that checked Mr. and Mrs. Parris in would later remember that they smiled at one another happily and even held hands as they climbed the stairs to their second-floor room—no. 214. The *Las Vegas Sun* January 8, 1967 issue reported:

> Deputy coroner Harvey Schnitzer reported the blast force was fantastic—scattering victims in an unbelievable manner. All of the victims were decapitated and one skull was found lying in an adjoining alley—it had

been blown through the roof and over the wall. The leg of a woman was found embedded in a wall.

It was as gruesome as it gets. The newspaper went on to say that all the victims were decapitated by the blast, and a woman's hand with wedding and engagement rings still on a finger was found. Like so many other murder–suicides, this was a crime without rhyme or reason. If there are answers, they are as obscure today, fifty years later, as they were on the night Richard James Parris fired into a bundle of fifty sticks of dynamite.

Happy Birthday

It's love that makes the World go round.

W. S. Gilbert

Everilda (Evie) Watson was happily celebrating a milestone—July 9, 2006, was her fiftieth birthday, and her husband, John, threw her a surprise birthday. He had also made arrangements for them to continue the celebration in Las Vegas. She was thrilled at the prospect of spending some time in Las Vegas, after which she would fly to Guatemala and visit her relatives; this was a perfect birthday.

Little did she know that her husband had been planning her murder for nearly a month. Retired high school math teacher Watson had complained to a friend that he believed Evie was thinking about divorcing him. This was bad enough, but the thought of her taking half their assets with her when she left was unbearable. That, he said, made him mad enough to kill her. Most damning of all, he boasted to his friend that he knew places where he could hide her body so that it would never be found. Now you may be wondering what kind of person talks, or even thinks, about such things. In the end, Watson's actions proved just what kind of a person he was.

The Watsons had scrimped and saved for decades. Between his teacher's salary and her cafeteria worker pay, they had raised three kids and somehow managed to squirrel away a nice little $1 million nest egg; that was not exactly chump change and John Watson meant to hang onto it. He would stop her at any cost. On July 10, he drove ahead to Las Vegas and rented a room at Circus Circus using his real name. Then, wearing a disguise and using the name "Joe Nunez," he checked into the two rooms at the Tuscany Suites he had booked a month earlier. The second room he said was for "Sal Nunez." In booking the rooms, Watson had been very specific about which ones he wanted—rooms 118 and 120. When told that room 120 was taken, Watson chose room 114 instead.

The next day, an average-looking woman made her way through a busy McCarran International terminal and out into the intense desert heat. She may have allowed herself to smile as she thought of the fun she and John were soon to have here. They had been married over twenty years and she thought she knew her husband very well; she did not. John Matthus Watson III smiled as he opened the door for her. Unsuspecting, she stepped through the doorway—the birthday celebration was set to begin. Everilda Watson would never be seen again.

A few days later, Watson drove home to Ontario, California, without Evie. He explained her absence by saying she had flown on to Guatemala where she planned to relocate. Evie, he said, had left behind credit cards, keys, and her wedding ring. This did not sound right. Alarmed, one of their sons filed a missing person report. Two days later, Watson was arrested in the disappearance when it was discovered that he was carrying fake identification in the name of Joseph Ernest Nunez, Jr.

The investigation into the disappearance of Everilda Watson continued with the discovery of blood in Watson's Jeep Grand Cherokee. He explained that Evie had cut her finger while opening a package. Watson had no explanation for having purchased a band saw, odor neutralizer, incense, bleach, anti-freeze, and odor-absorbent bags the day he said she went missing; neither could he explain Evie's blood that was in the carpet of that Tuscany hotel room, or her DNA in the shower drain of that room.

He was arrested and charged with the murder, kidnapping, and robbery of Everilda Watson. He would confess to shooting her and cutting her body up with the saw. In a confession letter written from his jail cell, Watson also told of cooking part of her body and eating it. Then he would claim that Evie had committed suicide. While in custody, he also told investigators that he had killed a hitchhiker in the 1960s and hidden the body.

On June 10, 2010, after deliberating for two hours, the jury found him guilty of first-degree murder. Watson begged for the death penalty, saying he had converted to Islam and wanted to correct punishment for his crime. "You don't get to pick your punishment," the judge admonished him. However, somebody was listening. In the penalty phase of his trial, the jury came back and sentenced Watson to death for his crime.

Four years later, he had a change of heart. He did not want to die. Claiming numerous errors during his trial and the penalty phase, he appealed his conviction to the Nevada Supreme Court. The court found against him; the death penalty would remain in place. Then, on June 13, 2019, Watson got another chance. Nine years after a jury found him guilty of first-degree murder, Clark County District Court Judge Michelle Leavitt overturned Watson's conviction and granted him a new trial because of an error on the part of his attorney. However, the Nevada Supreme Court will have to review Judge Leavitt's ruling first. At time of writing, no decision has been handed down.

Dancer

Las Vegas is the place for those in the entertainment industry to see and the place to be seen and make it big. So it was with dancer Debbie Flores-Narvaez, a beautiful and talented young woman who left Maryland for Las Vegas with high hopes. She had no formal dance training, but she had been a cheerleader for the Washington Redskins; she also had talent and big dreams. By early 2010, those dreams were coming true and she was living the Vegas lifestyle.

Debbie had danced her way from a go-go dancer at the Rain nightclub in the Palms to a stage role in the popular Fantasy Revue at the Luxor. She was in a relationship with dancer Jason Omar Griffith, who went by the professional name "Blu." He had an equally great gig in Cirque de Soleil's "The Beatles LOVE" at the Mirage.

It might have been perfect, if only Blu had been as committed to her as she was to him. He was not. There were other women, and this was something Debbie, whose loyalty was boundless, found difficult to accept. Yet the tempestuous on-again-off-again relationship continued. An abortion and later a violent argument in October 2010 changed everything between them. The fight ended with Debbie being kicked and thrown to the floor. Blu was arrested and charged with domestic violence. Now, the Puerto Rican beauty was finally through with him, but he came back with sweet words and lots of promises and they made up like they always did. The relationship resumed, and they continued seeing each other sporadically. Although it broke Debbie's heart to know that he could never be monogamous, she could never let go.

Debbie and Blu were among the *Dexter* fans that anxiously awaited each new episode of the hit Showtime TV series. With the season five finale of Dexter set to air thirteen days before Christmas 2010, they made plans to watch it together at Blu's place. However, when Debbie arrived, she discovered that Blu's roommate was also there. The show started and then they started to argue. The roommate did not want to be involved in their fight and left.

It was not like Debbie to be a no show. A dedicated dancer, she realized the importance of rehearsals, but she had blown the midnight rehearsal off without so much as a text. Likewise, she blew off the 5 p.m. Monday performance. This was not like someone whose dance career meant everything. Where was she? When an out-of-state friend learned of Debbie's no show, she realized that something had to be wrong. The woman called the Las Vegas Metropolitan Police Department and asked for their help in locating her friend. The last she had heard, Debbie was going to her ex-boyfriend's place to watch *Dexter*.

When questioned, the boyfriend knew nothing. Last he had seen her, she was fine and driving away in her Prism; they had not watched *Dexter* together, but when her roommate called the police to report Debbie and her car missing, she also told them about the plan to watch the television show. The Prism was found later that day, but there was no sign of Debbie Flores-Narvaez.

Days went by; friends and family continued to hope for her safe return. A joyless Christmas came and went. The days turned into weeks. Fliers and missing person posters of the vivacious Debbie were put out seeking the public's help in locating her. Surely someone knew something, and someone did.

Debbie Flores-Narvaez had been missing for twenty-four days when a witness came forward on January 5, 2011. The former girlfriend of Jason (Blu) Omar Griffith gave a damning statement concerning the disappearance of the dancer. On December 15, 2010, Blu had come to her place asking if he could store some things there for a while. She told him that her apartment was small, but if his stuff would fit in the closet or the patio, he was welcome to do so.

The next thing she knew, Griffith and a friend were unloading a large plastic tub from a U-Haul truck. Upon closer inspection, she noticed that the tub was filled with a dark-colored concrete. Curious, she asked him what was in the tub. He ignored her. She asked again; if he would not tell her what was in the tub, she was not about to let him store it at her place. "Debbie's in there," he said.

One look and she realized he was not joking; she was not going to let him keep that here. He and his friend lifted the tub back into the rental truck and left. Had he lied to her? What should she do? Would she meet the same fate if she told what she knew? That thought frightened her. It would be weeks before she finally came forward to tell her story and to share the name of Griffith's friend. Three days later, the friend was at the police department and asking for a deal. After assurances of leniency for his part in helping Griffith dispose of the remains, he began to talk and he knew every gruesome detail. What is more, he was willing to tell police where they could find the body, still encased in a plastic tub.

Debbie Flores-Narvaez, he said, came to Blu's place to watch *Dexter* on the night of December 12. Like they always did, Debbie and Blu started to fight. He left them to it at around 8.30 p.m. When he returned to the house hours later, Blu showed him Debbie's body and informed him that he had killed her accidentally. Now he needed to dispose of the body. They stuffed the corpse into a tub, filled it with concrete, and put it in the garage to harden overnight.

The next day, they rented a truck and moved the tub to the house of a friend who was out of the country. There, they found that the tub was leaking so they broke it open with a sledgehammer. Blu then took a hacksaw and sawed off both of Flores-Narvaez's legs. Finished, he placed the legs in a separate tub from the body and filled each with fresh concrete.

Testifying at his trial, Griffith said that during their relationship Debbie had harassed, stalked, threatened, and assaulted him. Debbie, he said, had brought on the argument that preceded her death by telling him she was pregnant again and needed an abortion. She then demanded that he stop seeing another dancer in the production. Her arm hit his face as she reached for her purse. He thought she was reaching for a gun and grabbed her around the neck; he killed her in self-defense.

After nine days of testimony and fourteen hours of jury deliberation, Griffith was convicted of second-degree murder in the death of Debbie Flores-Narvaez. In July 2014, Judge Kathleen Delaney handed down the maximum sentence—ten years to life imprisonment. "The responsibility for this toxic and ultimately tragic relationship continuing as long as it did was entirely yours. The only reason I can see was to satisfy your own narcissistic predisposition." Judge Delaney told Griffith.

As he was escorted from the courtroom, Griffith blew a kiss to his mother. His appeals were denied. At time of writing, Griffith is an inmate at Nevada's High Desert State Prison in Indian Springs, Nevada.

George Tiaffay

To the casual observer, a job in one of Las Vegas's large hotel casino resorts might seem like glamourous work, but anyone that has ever worked in the gaming industry knows that there are no easy jobs in Nevada's casinos; some are harder than others. Serving cocktails is one of those. The silver lining is the money, which is very good. Cocktail-waitressing can provide one with a six figure or more income, ensuring a better than average lifestyle. This is particularly true if a woman is clever, pleasant, exceptionally pretty, and working in a topnotch place.

At forty-six years of age, Shauna Tiaffay was just such a woman. By the time they reach their late forties, most women are hanging up their skimpy cocktail waitress uniforms, but not Shauna. She might not have been a fresh-faced twenty-something, but Shauna Tiaffay was very attractive and good at her job. She worked swing shift at the prestigious Palms and had been there since its grand opening in 2001. Maybe it was not the perfect shift for a wife and mother, but swing shift is generally where the most money is. Besides that, she loved her job and got along well with her co-workers.

She was friendly and outgoing, occasionally joining her co-workers for an after-shift drink. Casino culture is one in which after-shift drinks often lead to flirtations, affairs, and ultimately divorce. However, Shauna was not like that. They all knew Shauna's life revolved around her husband, George, and her daughter. He was the love of her life—a West Point grad and Las Vegas firefighter. In her eyes, he had been such a catch. Her daughter was an adorable little girl with the features of both her dark-eyed dad and her blonde mom. Shauna had never been happier.

Five years into their marriage, the rosy glow dimmed. Shauna began to see another side of George. Without provocation, he could turn mean, petty, and controlling. His behavior put their lives in turmoil. Shauna struggled to make their marriage better, but there was no peace or solace in their home. With George's constant barrage of hateful and demeaning words and the presence of a homeless man (Noel Stevens) doing odd jobs around their place, Shauna was uncomfortable in her own home. George was obviously on friendly terms with the man, but there was something about him that unnerved her. Perhaps deep within her, Shauna could sense the pure evil that lay beneath the surface of George's and Noel's odd friendship.

Finally, Shauna faced the truth; she was miserable in her marriage. George was too controlling. He was not the same man she married and he was never going to change. She made a decision as she was at a point where she could take no more. She rented an apartment and moved out. She would build a better life for herself and her daughter. As much as she still loved her husband, she had no intentions of ever going back to the abusive marriage. Yet George had other ideas. He did not want the marriage to be over and he certainly did not want a costly and a messy divorce.

On September 29, 2012, early Saturday morning, a full moon hung over Las Vegas. Those in the casino industry know just how weird people can get during a full moon; that Friday was no exception. It had been a long night. After eight hours of high heels and forced smiles, Shauna was exhausted. She only wanted to go home and sleep. She punched out at the Palm's time clock, changed into her street clothes, and headed home. Traffic was still light. It would take her about twenty minutes to drive the 9 miles west to her apartment in the affluent Summerlin area. In that time, she may have listened to music and made plans for the next day. Her daughter was with George, so Shauna would be able to sleep late and enjoy a lazy day.

Shauna unlocked the door of her Willowbrook apartment and stepped inside. She reached for the light. He sprang out of the shadows, startling her. She tried to fight, tried to escape. She was in top physical shape, but she was no match for his strength and the claw hammer he viciously wielded. Striking her again and again, he beat her to death there in the safety of her own home.

Several hours later George would discover Shauna's lifeless body when he brought their daughter home. Suspicion generally falls on the spouse of a murder victim, unless they have a very strong alibi, which George did. The previous day, his mother had watched his and Shauna's daughter while he worked a twenty-four-hour shift at the fire station. His was an airtight alibi. Investigators would have to look elsewhere for the killer.

The murder of Shauna Tiaffay was brutal and senseless. Television newscasters told the story; a woman was battered to death in her own home in a relatively safe area of town. The city was on edge. Where and when would the killer strike again? It is an interesting aspect of police work that many seemingly difficult cases are solved by a lucky break. So it was with the murder of Shauna Tiaffay. Two days after the murder, investigators received the tip that would break the case wide open.

A man called police to report that a friend of his had confessed to the killing of a woman with a hammer. He had said that he struck her so many times that he broke the hammer. The caller explained that his friend went by the street name of Greyhound, and he lived in a homeless campsite on the edge of the city.

When investigators finally located him, Greyhound admitted his name was Noel Stevens. However, he swore he knew nothing about Shauna Tiaffay's murder. Then how did he explain the dead woman's blood on pants they found at his campsite? Looking through Stevens's cell phone, they found the name "George." When asked, Stevens admitted George was his friend the firefighter. Investigators discovered the two of them had exchanged over eighty phone calls during the month of September.

Suddenly, George Tiaffay's airtight alibi was falling apart. His involvement in the murder of his wife was becoming clear. There was more damning evidence to come. Like other large businesses, Lowes has security cameras on the premises; it was this surveillance tape that caught George Tiaffay and Noel Stevens buying claw hammers and knives five days before the murder. It was all over. Noel Stevens confessed. George, he said, paid him $600 to kill Shauna, with the promise of more.

When he realized that detectives were looking into his involvement in his wife's murder, Tiaffay drove his truck into a concrete retaining wall at the edge of town. He was doing over 80 miles an hour. The failed suicide attempt put him in the hospital with minor injuries. When detectives came to the hospital and arrested George Tiaffay, it was every man for himself. With the promise that the death penalty would be off the table, Noel Stevens agreed to testify against George Tiaffay.

During his testimony, Stevens calmly told how Shauna had asked "Why are you doing this?" as he battered her with the hammer. When asked who told him to kill Shauna, he answered, "George." After fifteen hours of deliberation, the jury found George Tiaffay guilty of first-degree murder. His sentence was life without the possibility of parole. Noel Stevens was given a minimum forty-two years with the possibility of parole.

6
POLITICIANS

Governor Grant Sawyer and Nevada's Black Book

In January 1959, Democrat Grant Sawyer became Nevada's twenty-first governor. Even as Grant Sawyer and his family moved into the Governor's Mansion in Carson City, the mob was deeply entrenched in Las Vegas gambling. In 1960, Sawyer's administration issued an edict to the Gaming Commission; compile a list of those undesirables who should not be involved in Nevada's gaming industry. Thus the Black Book was created.

Once someone's name is entered into the Black Book, it prevents them from legally ever setting foot into a Nevada casino. There are two ways around inclusion in the Black Book—one can die, or one can petition the Nevada Gaming Commission for removal. As a fair warning, since the Black Book's creation in 1960, no one has successfully petitioned to have their name removed. There was a near miss when in 1990 Clark County Superior Court Judge Joseph Pavlowksi issued a preliminary ruling that Frank Rosenthal's name and photo should be removed from the Black Book. The ruling was appealed and overturned. Then there is Marshall Caifano, high-ranking Chicago mobster who legally changed his name to John Marshall when he moved to Las Vegas in 1951.

In 1963, John Marshall Caifano was the first person to be entered in Nevada's Black Book. He took his umbrage at being included in the Black Book to federal court in Las Vegas. Claiming his civil rights were violated because he was not permitted access to Nevada casinos, Caifano sued the Nevada Gaming Control board and sought $150,000 in damages. Caifano testified that the state had harassed him by throwing him out of a casino. Members of the gaming commission testified that Nevada needed such restrictions to keep the mob from taking over gambling in Nevada. The judge ruled against Caifano.

Still believing that he had the right to enter and exit any and all Nevada casinos at will, Caifano appealed. Once again, the court ruled against him stating, "Plaintiff's entry upon the gambling premises would present an emergency comparable to that presented by an animal running at large while suspected of being afflicted with foot-and-mouth disease." Governor Grant Sawyer issued a statement on the appeal court ruling.

> At the onset of Nevada's war against hoodlums and undesirables from other areas sojourning in this state, I said in regard to Marshall and all of the other Black Book figures, they could sue and be damned. Judge Crocker's decision vindicates my original feeling which I again re-emphasize by warning all persons of Marshall's ilk to stay out of Nevada's gambling areas.
>
> The continuation of exclusive control by the state is necessary, legal, and proper and will provide a further base for the strengthening of the industry and our general economy.

Still not happy, Caifano took his case to the United States Supreme Court who refused to hear it. That was the final word; Marshall (John Marshall) Caifano was not welcome in any of Nevada's gambling establishments.

In 1983, Anthony (Tony the Ant) Spilotro balked at his inclusion in the Black Book. He took his case to the Nevada Supreme Court, challenging the constitutionality of gaming regulations that barred him from entering a licensed Nevada gaming establishment and his inclusion in the Black Book. Spilotro maintained that his constitutional rights were being violated. The Nevada Supreme Court disagreed.

Thus far, only one woman has ever been placed in the Black Book; Sandra Kay Vaccaro's name was entered into the book in 1986 because of her part in her husband's slot cheating scam. The scam netted $1.6 million before the cheating duo and their gang of thieves was caught.

The Kefauver Committee

Back in television's infancy, screens were small, all presentations were shown in black and white, and there was not much to choose from when selecting one's viewing entertainment. In 1950, Tennessee Senator Estes Kefauver changed that with a resolution that would permit the Senate Committee on the Judiciary to investigate organized crime's role in interstate commerce. This was at a time when most adults had been contemporaries of (or had parents who had been contemporaries of) Eliot Ness, Al Capone, John Dillinger, Bugsy Siegel, and Bonnie and Clyde. They understood about those who flouted society's rules regarding criminal activity. Besides, J. Edgar Hoover was the director of the F.B.I. and had been since 1924.

The words organized crime got everyone's attention. Thus, the United States Senate Special Committee to Investigate Crime in Interstate Commerce began. The hearings were known as "the Kefauver hearings" and most would be televised, stopping the TV viewing starved public in its tracks. It was estimated that approximately 30 million people either watched on TV or listened to the hearings on their radios.

With Senator Kefauver as the committee chair, the hearings took place across the U.S. in fourteen major cities. Over 600 witnesses testified. One of those subpoenaed was Virginia Hill, a mob party girl and former flame of Benjamin (Bugsy) Siegel. Wearing a big floppy hat, the better to shield her face from cameras, Hill took the stand and claimed not to know anything about organized crime. Her testimony was some of the most colorful of the entire hearing.

On November 15, 1950, the Kefauver Committee came to federal courthouse and post office in Las Vegas. Among those subpoenaed was Wilbur Clark, front man for the Desert Inn; Clifford Jones, Nevada lieutenant governor; Moe Dalitz, owner of the Desert Inn; and Moe Sedway, manager of the Flamingo Hotel, who testified about his health ailments at the hearings. "You see what it got for me, three coronaries and ulcers," he said. "We don't get as rich as you think we do. This is hard work. I work pretty hard in this business." As far as his health went, Sedway was probably telling the truth. He died two years later of natural causes.

Having it Both Ways

Clifford A. Jones was Nevada's twentieth lieutenant governor. He served two terms from 1947 to 1954. Jones, whose nickname was "Big Juice," was also co-owner of the mob affiliated Thunderbird casino. This was the reason he was subpoenaed to testify before the Kefauver Committee.

At one point during the hearing, Jones was asked what he thought about so many people involved in Las Vegas casinos having criminal records. "I would say that I believe as long as they conduct themselves properly that I think there is probably no harm comes to it."

Jones admitted that he owned 11 percent stock in the Thunderbird but had not received money from it since its 1948 opening. Yet he had stock in other casinos. He then told the committee that he had received $12,000 that year from his 1 percent in the Golden Nugget casino and $14,000 from the 5 percent in the Pioneer casino. That was a pretty good haul in the early 1950s.

Clifford A. Jones's political career came crashing down when newspaper man Hank Greenspun hired a man to impersonate a prospective buyer and surreptitiously record conversations with Jones and others Las Vegas movers and shakers.

Fearing that the federal government would take over the regulation of Nevada casinos with the mob's involvement at the Thunderbird, Governor Charles Russell wisely asked the legislature to create a regulatory board. The Nevada State Gaming Control Board was approved in 1955, and Clifford A. Jones saw his gaming license revoked.

Great Idea, Oscar Goodman!

Las Vegas has earned its reputation as a city that is continually tearing down and rebuilding. Mega resorts are built and rebuilt. Any old building that happens to be in the way of progress is summarily bulldozed down to the ground to make way for the new.

This did not happen to the old federal courthouse and post office on Stewart Street in downtown Las Vegas. In 2000, the federal government sold the building to the city of Las Vegas for $1, but there was a catch; the city was on the hook to restore the building to its original look and it had to be used for cultural purposes.

Mayor Oscar Goodman, former mob attorney, whose clients included people like Tony Spilotro, had a brilliant idea in 2002; his honor suggested the building be repurposed as a mob museum. Politics being what they are, not everyone was onboard with the idea.

Yet you cannot keep a good idea down. The "Mob Museum," officially known as the National Museum of Organized Crime and Law Enforcement, opened its doors on Valentine's Day (anniversary of the St. Valentine's Day Massacre) 2012. The museum is dedicated to sharing artifacts and history of organized crime in the U.S. and of law enforcement. It is located at 300 Stewart Avenue in downtown Las Vegas. If you have not visited it yet, you are missing out.

The Senator and the Shyster

He was a thug out of Chicago, an enforcer for Al Capone. Yet as the West Coast representative of IATSE (International Alliance for Theatrical Stage Employees), Willie Bioff became a bigshot in 1930s Hollywood. He was not actually affiliated with the union, but it was a way into extorting millions of dollars from Hollywood movie studios for his bosses, who controlled the corrupt unions. He was living so large that others took notice; the IRS wondered why Willie neglected to pay taxes on his nice salary.

When he was arrested, Bioff avoided a long prison sentence for tax evasion and racketeering by turning on his friends. Willie talked and he told anything and everything that would keep him clear of a prison cell. Johnny Rosselli and Frank Nitti were among the friends that Willie turned on. Nitti committed suicide as a result of Willie's testimony. Rosselli remembered and he would see that one day, Willie Bioff paid.

With a reduced sentence behind him, Bioff was released and fled Chicago for Arizona's sunnier clime. In a new location with a new name, Willie was ready for a new start. He would take his wife's maiden name, Nelson, and from then on be known as William Nelson.

Along the way, he met Arizona Senator Barry Goldwater and the two became friends. He even donated and helped with Goldwater's re-election campaign. Then, he went to work for Gus Greenbaum at the Riviera.

When the mob heard that Willie was working at the Riviera, they let Gus know they wanted Willie fired as soon as possible, but Gus was stubborn. He liked the man he knew as William Nelson. He refused. So Willie continued working as entertainment director at the Riviera. Like Gus, he had a home in Phoenix and visited there often. According to one story, it was his good friend Senator Goldwater who flew Willie Bioff home in his private plane in 1955, which turned out to be the last time for Bioff.

On November 4, 1955, Willie walked out the front door and got into his pickup truck. He turned the key and pressed on the starter. The dynamite explosion rocked the neighborhood, sending bits of Bioff from one end to the other. The killer was never caught.

In a 1963 interview, Senator Goldwater denied knowing Bioff well. He was only an acquaintance, he knew him as William Nelson, Goldwater told reporters. Goldwater was a 1964 presidential candidate and although he had known both Greenbaum and Bioff, he denied knowing they were affiliated with the mob.

Operation G-String

> *"I didn't vote for the Patriot Act to allow the FBI to go after strip-club owners,"*
>
> *Nevada Rep. Shelley Berkley*

The mob might be long gone and skimming is a thing of the past, but sadly, crooked politicians and corruption are not. It all began because the owners of two Las Vegas strip clubs (Cheetahs and Crazy Horse Too) wanted to get rid of local no touch laws that were eventually repealed, but not before a slew of local politicians were swept up in the F.B.I.'s undercover net.

Based on their promises, we elect our politicians on what they can do for us, the average citizen. Most are honorable honest people who really do want to make our world a better place, but not all of them do; some of them are greedy self-serving people who simply want to increase their net worth. Clark County has seven commissioners, one for each district. The commissioners serve a four-year term. In 2002, some of them crossed the line in helping strip club owner Michael Galardi.

As Galardi fought to keep his dancer's free of the no-touch restrictions, he upped the ante by securing the services of Erin Kenny, a Clark County commissioner, who had served a term in the Nevada Assembly, and was the Democratic nominee for Nevada Lieutenant Governor, Mary Kincaid-Chauncey, Clark County commissioner and Clark County commissioner Dario Herrera, Clark County Commissioner Mark Matthew Malone.

While listening in on phone conversations, the F.B.I. heard Commissioner Erin Kenny say just before the 2002 elections, "Tell me what I've got to do, but I've got to have money from him ... I'm on my knees begging."

After an extensive undercover operation dubbed Operation G-String, the F.B.I. said that the commissioners used their public offices to further the interests of Michael Galardi, a strip club owner in Las Vegas. They solicited and accepted money, property, and services directly from Galardi and through co-defendant Lance Malone, another former county commissioner. The evidence demonstrated that members of the conspiracy concealed the payments they received from Galardi and failed to disclose the payments as required by law and their fiduciary duties as county commissioners. Needless to say, their political careers were kaput. They all served sentences at federal prison, came back to Las Vegas, and are living happily ever after.

J. F. K. Puts a Good Word in for Frankie

In 1963, Frank Sinatra was up to his eyeballs in trouble in the northern part of Nevada. The crooner who supposedly owned the Cal-Neva Lodge at Lake Tahoe was guilty of a big no-no in Nevada gaming; he was happily permitting gangster Sam Giancana access to his casino since they were pals.

Mobster Giancana liked to boast that he owned Las Vegas, and indeed, he had a hand in a lot of the city's real estate activity. However, he also had a girlfriend, Phyllis McGuire of the McGuire Sisters singing group and she was appearing at the Cal-Neva; being infatuated, where else would he be?

While running for president in February 1960, John F. Kennedy came to Las Vegas to hobnob with political pals and to raise money. While in Vegas, Kennedy enjoyed a performance by the Rat Pack (Frank Sinatra, Sammy Davis, Jr., Dean Martin, Peter Lawford, and Joey Bishop) at the Sands. Lawford was married to Kennedy's sister Pat, so they were all friends. During the sold-out show, the Rat Pack did what was expected; they asked their audience to contribute to Kennedy's campaign.

The first step toward cleaning the mob out of Las Vegas came in 1960 when Nevada's gaming regulators created the Black Book. Those with obvious underworld connections would not be licensed and certainly would not be permitted entrance to the casinos. Kennedy was elected president of the U.S. and Frank Sinatra owned the Cal-Neva at Lake Tahoe.

There were so many tall pines at Crystal Bay Tahoe and just as many tall tales of clandestine meetings at the Cal-Neva between Kennedy and blonde sex symbol actress Marilyn Monroe. Yet what really was catching F.B.I. attention was Sam Giancana and how he freely roamed the property. When informed of this transgression, Nevada gaming regulators came down on Frankie, who was breaking the rules.

They were ready to yank Sinatra's license. Instead of being contrite, he cried to his friend, the president. In September 1963, J. F. K. was in Las Vegas heading up his re-election bid. In his book, *Hang Tough*, former Nevada Governor Grant Sawyer says that as he and President Kennedy rode together toward the Las Vegas Convention Center, Kennedy asked, "What are you guys doing to my friend Frank Sinatra?"

Sawyer replied, "Mr. President, I'll try to take care of things here in Nevada, and I wish you luck on the national level." Two months later, Kennedy was assassinated and Frankie lost his license, but it was only temporary; after the Democrats angered and rejected him, Frankie felt betrayed, so he switched sides and became a Republican. Eventually, he was able to call on his two new friends—Paul Laxalt in the Nevada Governor's Mansion, and President Ronald Reagan in the White House.

Laxalt believed that Sinatra was beneficial to the state of Nevada, and Reagan, like Sinatra, was a member of the entertainment industry. Reagan is the only U.S. president to have starred in his own Las Vegas floor show.

Before Donald Trump was elected in 2016, Ronald Reagan was the only movie and TV star president, and he was listed as Sinatra's character reference in an application for approval as Caesars Palace's vice-president of entertainment. It is hard to discount the value of a sitting president's endorsement. The vote to approve was 4-1; just like that, Sinatra was licensed. Sinatra died on May 14, 1998. The next night, all the lights along the Strip were dimmed in his honor—talk about having friends in high places.

Murder–Suicide in a Retirement Mecca

Mesquite is 80 miles northeast, and a world apart, from Las Vegas. A far smaller community within the Mojave Desert, Mesquite is slower-paced and considered safer than the sprawling Las Vegas. Retirees are fast catching on. Retired police officers, Bill and Donna Fairchild came to Mesquite in 1999 after retiring from the Denver Police Department. She was forty; he was ten years older.

The Fairchilds eventually bought a stucco-style desert home complete with swimming pool and palm trees on Arguello Drive, in the all new gated Vista Del Lagos golf course community. Looking forward to living in the warmer desert climate, they happily settled in. Outgoing and attractive, they quickly made friends, who referred to them as Barbie and Ken. This was not meant as denigration, but rather as acknowledgment of the couple's vitality and good looks. While Donna busied herself with politics, Bill worked part-time at the Mesquite Recreation Center. Life was good, and then it was not. In January 2011, the 911 call was brief, lasting only twelve seconds. In it, the woman's voice explained, "We're in the bedroom, the front door is unlocked, and I'm post suicide."

Officers found Mr. and Mrs. Fairchild minutes later. A 9-mm gun was in her hand and a bullet had struck them in the head, ending their lives. She had killed him in his sleep. Then, she waited an hour to take her own life, but why did she do it? Unravelling a murder–suicide is not always possible. No one could imagine why Donna would do such a thing. Her best friend had had lunch with her the day before and did not notice any telltale signs of the tragedy that was to come. All too often people do not.

Donna left a note for her mother and a note for her friend, telling her how to disperse of her jewelry and other personal belongings, offered no explanation beyond the classic "I'm sorry." Donna was a Mesquite councilwoman. She had made plans to run for mayor. Under investigation for a $94 expense claim, she may have dreaded the embarrassment of resignation that surely would have followed. Maybe the couple had faced marital issues. Investigators ruled the case closed and life went on in the gated golf course community in Mesquite.

Judge Claiborne, Joe Conforte, and Joseph Yablonsky
the King of the Sting

In May 2019, Joseph Yablonsky died in Florida at the age of ninety. Yablonsky was a former F.B.I. agent assigned to the F.B.I. Las Vegas field office in 1980. Believing that the mob was still fully entrenched in the gaming industry and the skim, he immediately let it be known that he was ready to take on the underworld.

When he retired as special agent in charge of the Las Vegas field office in December 1983, Yablonsky had made his share of enemies and friends. He had worked undercover helping to take down one criminal after another, but it was on the word of Mustang Ranch brothel owner Joe Conforte that Yablonsky zeroed in on Judge Harry Claiborne, focusing his attention on putting the corrupt Claiborne behind bars. Never mind what others may have thought, Yablonsky believed Claiborne was crooked.

As an attorney, Harry Claiborne had represented many celebrities and underworld figures during his career. Judy Garland hired him as her divorce attorney, as did Carol Burnett. His clients had included Bugsy Siegel, Benny Binion, and Lefty Rosenthal. Stars such as Frank Sinatra and Dean Martin called him their attorney. In 1978, President Jimmy Carter appointed Claiborne to the United States District Court for the District of Nevada. He would hold this post from 1980 until 1986.

Joe Conforte was well-known in Northern Nevada where he and his wife, Sally, had operated the Mustang Ranch brothel, 20 miles east of Reno, since 1971. Conforte was the impetus for Yablonsky's take down of Judge Claiborne. The sordid saga began in 1977 when Joe Conforte and his now ex-wife, Sally, were arrested on ten counts of income tax evasion. Sally got a hefty fine. In addition to a hefty fine, Joe would have to do some jail time. He appealed and lost. He fled to Brazil. While there, Conforte contacted the F.B.I., wanting to make a deal. He would give feds the names of those officials he had bribed in exchange for reduced fees and charges. Joseph Yablonsky saw Judge Harry Claiborne's name on that list and wanted the deal. Joe Conforte claimed to have given Claiborne $85,000 in bribes.

Eight years later, the Nevada Supreme agreed that Claiborne could resume practicing law in Nevada. The court also criticized the F.B.I. investigators and prosecutors for what it found were "questionable investigative and prosecutorial motivations, as well as anomalous and arguably unfair practices that pervade the record of this matter since its inception."

Claiborne was convicted of tax evasion and sentenced to two years in prison. He was the first federal judge to be sent to prison. He served seventeen months and released in 1987. On January 19, 2004, in failing health, eighty-six-year-old Claiborne committed suicide. Joe Conforte died in Brazil in March 2019. He was ninety-three years old.

EPILOGUE

There can never really be an end. Human nature being what it is, crime will be with us for as long as humans reside on earth. Sociologists tell us the causations of crime and psychologists give us insight into criminal behavior, and laypeople like me write about crime. One question I have asked myself while writing this book is this—would these people have committed these crimes in another place, for instance in Broken Bow, Nebraska? Was location a factor in these crimes being committed? As a layperson, I have come to the conclusion that the answer to the first question is "probably not." However, I have to say "yes" in answer to the second question, especially when looking at mob involved crimes.

At the onset, I said that Las Vegas is fabulous and it is. Las Vegas is a city that attracts all sorts of people, each with a myriad of dreams and wants and needs. Some take their dreams and go far like former Las Vegas Mayor Oscar Goodman, who is probably one of the best mayors the city has ever elected. Others shed their humanity like a snake sheds its skin and let their dreams take them to a dark place of madness from which there is no escape. While we think of dreams, let us not forget those of the innocent victims whose dreams surely did not included the fates they met—victims who often times really did happen to be in the wrong place at the wrong time.

Writing this book has been an adventure for me—not always an easy adventure but an adventure nonetheless. Let me close here by saying that I sincerely hope that you dear reader, have found the resulting book an informative and entertaining adventure.

BIBLIOGRAPHY

BOOKS

Assael, S., *The Murder of Sonny Liston* (Blue Rider Press, October 18, 2016)

Brill, S., *The Teamsters* (Simon & Schuster, New York, New York)

Brown, D. H., *Money, Mob and Influence in Harry Reid's Nevada* (Independent Publishing, 2015)

Capote, T., *In Cold Blood* (Vintage, February 1, 1994)

Cole, N., *Angel on My Shoulder: An Autobiography* (Grand Central Publishing, November 14, 2000)

Conforte, J. and Toll, D., *Breaks, Brains and Balls: The Story of Joe Conforte and the Fabulous Mustang Ranch* (Gold Hill Publishing Co., Inc., January 27, 2011)

Cullotta, F. and Griffin, D. N., *The Rise and Fall of a Casino Mobster: the Tony Spilotro Story Through a Hitman's Eyes* (Wild Blue Press, 2017)

Denton, S. and Morris, R., *The Money and the Power: The Making of Las Vegas and its Hold on America 1947–2000* (Alfred A. Knopf, New York, 2001)

Dickey, R., *Greyhound to Vegas* (St. Margaret Publishers, 2011)

Farrell, R. A. and Case, C., *The Black Book and the Mob: The Untold Story of the Control of Nevada's Casinos* (University of Wisconsin Press, 1995)

Fischer, S., *When the Mob Ran Las Vegas* (Berkline Press, 2005)

Fleeman, M., *If I Die* (St. Martin's Paperbacks, January 2002)

Gage, N., *Mafia, U.S.A.* (Playboy Press, 1972)

Griffin, D. N., *The Battle for Las Vegas: The Law VS. The Mob* (Huntington Press, Las Vegas, 2006)

Hopkins, H. and Sugerman, D., *No One Here Gets Out Alive* (Grand Central Publishing, New York, New York, 1980)

Kevlin, T. A., *Headless Man in Topless Bar* (Dog Ear Publishing, Indianapolis, IN, 2007)

Moe, A., *Nevada's Golden Age of Gambling*

Moehring, E. P., *Resort City in the Sunbelt Las Vegas, 1930–1970* (University of Nevada Press Reno, Las Vegas, 1989)

Moehring, E. P. and Green, M. S., *Las Vegas: A Centennial History* (University of Nevada Press Reno, Nevada, 2005)

Paher, S. W., *Las Vegas, As It Began, As It Grew* (Nevada Publishing, July 6, 1971)

Puit, G., *Fire in the Desert: The True Story of the Craig Titus-Kelly Ryan Murder Mystery* (Stephens Press LLC, December 1, 2006)

Puit, G., *Witch: The Bone-Chilling True Story of US Murderer Brookey Lee West* (Ebury Press, October 15, 2012)

Reid, E., *The Mistress and the Mafia: The Virginia Hill Story* (Bantam Books, 1974)

Reid, E. and Ovid, D., *The Green Felt Jungle* (Ishi Press International, 2010)

Roemer, Jr., W. F., *The Enforcer: Spilotro—The Chicago Mob's Man Over Las Vegas* (Donald I. Fine, 1994)

Rothman, H., *Neon Metropolis: How Las Vegas Started the Twenty-first Century* (Routledge, February 22, 2002)

Sawyer, G., *Hang Tough: An Activist in the Governor's Mansion* (University of Nevada Oral History, October 1, 1993)

Schwartz, D. G., *Grandissimo: The First Emperor of Las Vegas: How Jay Sarno Won a Casino Empire, Lost it, and Inspired Modern Las Vegas* (Winchester Books, October 2013)

Scott, C., *The Killing of Tupac Shakur* (Huntington Press, Las Vegas, October 1, 2002)

Server, L., *Handsome Johnny: The Life and Death of Johnny Rosselli; Gentleman Gangster, Hollywood Producer, CIA Assassin* (St. Martin's Press, November 13, 2018)

Smith, J., *Of Rats and Men: Oscar Goodman's Life from Mob Mouthpiece to Mayor of Las Vegas* (Huntington Press, Las Vegas, 2012)

Sutton, W. and Linn, E., *Where the Money Was: Memoirs of a Bank Robber* (Viking Press, 1976)

Vernetti, M., *Lies Within Lies: The Betrayal of Nevada Judge Harry Claiborne*

Wilkerson, W. R. III, *The Man Who Invented Las Vegas* (January 2000)

MAGAZINES

Crandall, J. J. and Harrod, R., "Ghostly Gunslingers: The Postmortem Lives of the Kiel Brothers, Nevada's First Frontiersmen," *Cambridge Archeological Journal* (April 2014)